Front Yard Gardens

Front Yard Gardens

Growing More Than Grass

Liz Primeau

■

photography by

Andrew Leyerle

FIREFLY BOOKS

A Firefly Book

Published by Firefly Books Ltd. 2003

Second printing 2003

National Library of Canada Cataloguing in Publication Data

Primeau, Liz
Front yard gardens : growing more than grass / Liz Primeau.

Includes index.
ISBN 1-55297-665-3 (bound). — ISBN 1-55297-710-2 (pbk.)
1. Gardening.   2. Landscape gardening.   I. Title.
SB454.P75 2003   635.9'67   C2002-905273-4

Publisher Cataloging-in-Publication Data (U.S)
(Library of Congress Standards)

Primeau, Liz.
   Front yard gardens : growing more than grass / Liz Primeau.
      —1st pbk. ed.
[232] p. : col. photos. ; cm.
Includes index.
Summary: How to transform a front yard from grass to a garden.
Includes garden styles, tips on creating and maintaining the garden, planting suggestions and examples of more than
70 front yard gardens across North America.
ISBN 1-55297-665-3   ISBN 1-55297-710-2 (pbk.)
1. Gardens — North America.   2. Landscape gardening.   I. Title.
635.9 21 SB473.P75 2003

Published in Canada in 2003 by
Firefly Books Ltd.
3680 Victoria Park Avenue
Toronto, Ontario M2H 3K1

Published in the United States 2003 by
Firefly Books (U.S.) Inc.
P.O. Box 1338, Ellicott Station
Buffalo, New York 14205

Design: Counterpunch/Linda Gustafson
Managing Editor: Charis Cotter
Photo Research: Vivien Leong

Printed and bound in Canada by Friesens, Altona, Manitoba

The Publisher acknowledges the financial support of the Government of Canada
through the Book Publishing Industry Development Program for its publishing activities.

To Uncle Ren

Acknowledgements

Even though it's the author who gets her name on the cover, it takes a great many people to produce a book, and even more to inspire it. Without innovative gardeners bold enough to move into the front yard from the back, I wouldn't have had a book. The ones on these pages spent hours telling me about their experiences and made the research fun as well as educational – my interview tapes attest to that.

Andrew Leyerle, the principal photographer, matched my enthusiasm for the project from the moment we first discussed it. He found many of the gardens while on his travels, and spent endless hours waiting for just the right light or for an errant breeze to die down so he could catch their beauty on film. I thank him for his dedication and his patience. Thanks also to the additional photographers who contributed to the book and rounded out its content.

Charis Cotter, who edited my words and steered the project through the trauma of production, knew exactly when to be flattering and when to be firm, and how to change her mind graciously when the situation warranted it. I also appreciate the humor with which she responded to my e-mails, which sometimes nearly reached chapter length.

Designer Linda Gustafson is another who adopted my project enthusiastically and made it her own. She's given my words and Andrew's photographs the perfect setting and classy look I was hoping for.

Thanks also to Ross Pettigrew of the Pest Management Regulatory Agency and Ken Pavely of Landscape Ontario, who both read over and commented on the chart on page 23, and to Len Ritter of Guelph University's department of environmental biology, who helped me get a fix on the dangers of pesticides in our world.

Lionel Koffler, Michael Worek and Françoise Vulpe at Firefly listened when I said there was a book in front yard gardens, even if other publishers were skeptical. For their support I am sincerely grateful, for without it this book wouldn't exist.

He may appear last, but he's never least: Chris keeps me laughing and he never complains, even when he doesn't get the credit he deserves for helping me create the garden of my dreams.

Liz Primeau
November, 2002

Contents

Chapter One

Why We Mow

Back in the fifties, a neighbor used to joke that his lawn – without a doubt the greenest, thickest, most perfect one on the street – cost him $5,000 every summer.

This was a wild exaggeration, of course, but we got the point. The bucks went mostly for water, but a considerable amount was consumed by fertilizer, pesticides and herbicides, spring and fall top-dressing, a bag or two of seed to spruce up bare areas and a few rolls of sod to replace grass consumed by white grubs.

As he unloaded lawn-care supplies from his trunk after a visit to the local nursery on Saturday mornings, my neighbor would laugh about his obsession to anyone within hearing distance, poking a little fun at himself. But his jokes were telling. He was inordinately proud of his lawn, and spent hours cutting or grooming it. He tended to its every complaint with the attention of a doting mother to a sick child. I doubt if our neighbor ever figured out exactly how much his thick carpet of turf cost. It remained lush and deep green all season, despite grass's tendency to become dormant in mid-summer, and in spite of the occasional all-season drought. Drought he considered nature's biggest challenge, an occasion to rise to with the fervor of a warrior

The beautiful lawn and gardens at Stowe Landscape School in Buckingham, England, were designed by William Kent in the 1730s, and miraculously survive today. Kent and Capability Brown revolutionized landscape design in the eighteenth century by advocating expanses of "natural" lawns like this, dotted with copses of trees.

whose turf, literally, had been invaded. He and his grass always triumphed. The texture was always soft, with blades thicker than the tufts in my new plush broadloom. His lawn was so perfect that the kids in the neighborhood preferred it to their jungle gyms for afternoon play. Our neighbor – a kind man, really – gritted his teeth and looked the other way as they somersaulted and tumbled on its velvety surface. His lawn was a prized possession he'd rather admire than use.

Even in my naive youth I suspected our neighbor was lording it over us. But this was the fifties, and the lawn was king. The rest of us on the street, newly married suburbanites with our first homes, actually envied him – he'd reached a level of lawn nirvana we couldn't yet achieve, but we would one day. We couldn't imagine it any other way.

Were lawns the law? They might as well have been. At the very least there was an unwritten rule that grass would be the feature of the front yard, backed by evergreen foundation plantings and maybe a shade tree in the center of the lawn. Neighbors with patchy or unmown grass were frowned upon, or worse. The unspoken threat of a call to the bylaw officer always hung in the air. The appearance of a single dandelion made us shudder and offer to loan the culprit a can of our most lethal herbicide – after all, we had standards to uphold.

On occasion we veered a degree or two from total conformity: for example, the island shrub bed planted by an eccentric neighbor to replace the yews and junipers under the picture window was considered a blatant example of front-yard rebellion, until we decided we liked the effect and began to copy the idea.

But none of us could part with our lawns. They were as necessary to the suburban landscape as our cars. Our neighborhood, in fact, was little different from any other in North America. For nearly a century the groomed front lawn had been *de rigueur* on almost every street on this continent. At last count, more than 24 million acres of lawn grow in North America, and this doesn't include grasslands and areas such as highway embankments. The care and feeding of grass has become a multibillion-dollar business for lawn-care companies and for manufacturers of pesticides, herbicides, fertilizers, lawn mowers and all the related equipment. The lawn itself is an institution, gracing more than suburban subdivisions. Highway cloverleafs have lawns, as do cemeteries, golf courses and the large corporations that take up acres of land on the outskirts of cities.

Our Love of Lawns: Nature or Nurture?

Where did our love of grass come from? Why are we so obsessed with lawns? One theory was put forward a few years ago by Dr. John Falk, an ecologist and former special assistant at the Smithsonian Institution, as the result of research and surveys conducted since 1978. He calls it the Savanna Syndrome. In his view, our love of grass dates back to the time when humans roamed the savannas of Africa in search of food. We preferred to forage on grassy plains dotted with copses of trees because they offered protection from predators, which we could easily spot as they crept up on us in the short grass. Over the millennia, this was encoded in our DNA.

Of course, not a word of this can be proven, although many psychologists agree that humans have an innate preference for open spaces that provide "legibility," which means an environment that's clear and easily understood. Many non-professionals among us firmly believe our love of grass – and of gardening in general – is an instinctive throwback to our pastoral roots or to our need to prove our superiority over nature. I confess to having expounded on these theories more than once myself. I swear my own early interest in gardening is genetic (I come from a long line of farmers), and I wasn't the only one on our street to recognize that our neighbor's obsession with his grass revealed his need for control.

But we need only look back in history to realize that cultivation of the land in general has always reflected our need to understand and control nature, if only to survive. The ancient walled gardens of Persia were physical and psychological sanctuaries from the harsh environment beyond; medieval gardens, up to and including the cottage gardens of the early eighteenth century, were necessary for sustenance and survival as the source of food and herbs both culinary and medicinal. If any grass grew in those tiny closely planted cottage gardens, the goats ate it for lunch.

The North American lawn as we know it has a more recent history, as well as a more prosaic one. Our fascination with grass has its modern roots in seventeenth-century France's much-admired formal gardens of André Le Nôtre's Versailles, with their *tapis verts*, or small green carpets of grass, built into a tight structure of beds designed to prove that man was a better landscape architect than nature. This style was copied by the English until the eighteenth century, when William Kent and Capability Brown revolutionized landscape design: in their view, nature was a power to be embraced, not controlled, and soon the manor houses of England were surrounded with great greenswards of grass that swept right up to the front doors and off to the horizon. These landscapes were considered natural, but in the end were just more cultivated lawn.

The Landscape Movement: Upper-Class Grass

Capability Brown, in particular (his real name was Lancelot, but he was nicknamed Capability because of his constant reference to a site's "capabilities"), liked the grand vision. He spared no client's expense to recontour land and uproot trees (even tearing down houses he considered unnecessary) to make smooth surfaces for carpets of grass, scythed, rolled,

Both the hospital and the formal gardens at Royal Hospital Kilmainham, in Dublin, Ireland, have their origins in French style. The hospital, founded in 1680 to care for old soldiers, was inspired by Louis XIV's Les Invalides, the garden by Le Nôtre's design for Versailles.

Thomas Jefferson was one of the first Americans to grow an English-style lawn on his estate, Monticello, in Virginia. The view from the west front of the mansion is shown above in an 1825 painting by Jane Braddick Peticolas.

swept and manured into lush and perfect lawns. Sound familiar? The influence of the garden park is also evident on many of today's large suburban estates, where expanses of lawn set off with trees seem to be the only treatment the landscape architect can envision for a vast space.

This was the peak of the Landscape Movement in England, but like many other landscape styles it was accessible only to the upper classes, who had both the property and the money to care for such large areas of grass. This didn't discourage immigrants to the New World, who

brought this vision of endless lawns with them. Hopeful that it would reflect the riches and class such landscapes suggested, the most affluent among the colonists borrowed the approach for their new but more modest land holdings, despite the fact that conditions here did not favor the growth of the fine lawn grasses of England. Highly placed travelers to England also admired the style and brought it back to North America, the illustrious Thomas Jefferson among them. He especially admired Moor Park, a Brown-designed landscape in Hertfordshire, England, and used ideas from it on the grounds of his home, Monticello, in Virginia. The extensive, tiered grass grounds around the University of Virginia's Jeffersonian complex, built as part of his vision of education in America, is still known as "The Lawn" to graduates and students alike.

Although lawns had a presence in North America as the country entered the nineteenth century, they were still a privilege of the wealthy. Pioneers and farmers without the resources or the time for decorative gardening had to remain content with packed-dirt front yards, if they had any yard at all, swept daily to keep the dust down. But the seed was sown: a spacious, rich lawn had become a status symbol, and the desire for one spread to the budding middle class.

The Nineteenth Century:
A Lawn for Every Yard

After the Industrial Revolution and the American Civil War, the lawn really took hold as a landscape ideal in North America. The fuels used by the machines of the new manufacturing industries produced heavy pollution in urban centers, causing the middle class to seek more pastoral surroundings beyond city boundaries. Railways, streetcars and trolley lines were expanded, and by the late 1800s the suburb, with its detached houses and larger lots, was part of North American life.

In many of the suburbs, as well as in small towns, setbacks of 25 feet or more from house to street began to be the law. This was a huge change from the older city houses, built to abut almost directly onto the street. In smaller communities in New England, village centers began to metamorphose from "commons" into "greens." Formerly untidy packed-earth locations for military drills, hangings, town fairs and other gatherings of the townsfolk, they became parks with mowed lawns and trees, and the activities that were too hard on the grass had to move elsewhere.

With more leisure time available, lawn sports became fashionable, and games like croquet and lawn tennis cemented the value of a thick, well-groomed lawn as a base for family activities. Activities like lawn bowling and golf were also becoming popular, and required a strong turf to play on.

The upkeep of grass requires labor, but luckily Edward Budding had come to the rescue, reducing the need for

By the late nineteenth century, the first clunky lawn mowers had been streamlined so that even "delicate" young girls could use them, as illustrated in this ad for Excelsior mowers.

hired help to scythe the grass: in 1830 he'd invented a rather bulky lawn mower, useful for moderately sized plots. It wasn't as useful as it might have been, however, because it required two strong arms to push it. By the 1870s he'd streamlined it so that even a "delicate" woman could operate it — advertisements eager to illustrate this showed children and women in their Sunday best mowing the lawn while the rest of the family played croquet or lawn tennis in the background. By this time hoses, sprinklers and city water supplies were also available to assist in the proper care of grass.

Lawns need grass seed, too, and agricultural conditions had taken care of this requirement as well, if by default. In the east, where lawns were most seen, our indigenous grasses had, sadly, pretty well disappeared, grazed to near-extinction by the colonists' cattle, sheep and goats. These grasses were replaced by European imports brought in with the idea that they would make good meadows for grazing, with some seeds arriving as stowaways in ships' ballast. The incongruously named Bermuda grass and Kentucky bluegrass, for example (the first is native to Africa, the second to the Middle East), became so common they're considered native grasses by many.

The Democratic Lawn

These influences on the developments of the North American lawn were evolutionary, even passive, compared to the direct hit of landscape architect Frederick Law Olmsted, the man who in the mid-1800s designed Montreal's Mount Royal Park and New York's Central Park in the manner of England's grand estates. In 1869 Olmsted was commissioned to plan the new suburb of Riverside, Illinois, near Chicago, and he carried the torch for the lawn. He designed a neighborhood of curving streets quite unlike the grid pattern prevalent in most cities, and he stipulated that each house was to be set back 30 feet from the road. No garden walls or fences were allowed, since he felt they made a row of homes look like "a series of private madhouses." Each property had to have at least one tree, plus the lawn, which was to blend with the neighbors' on each side as if they were one.

Riverside, in effect, was planned to resemble one great park, with its grounds open and appreciated by all. This was a departure from the grand estates of England, each of which was clearly the property of one person, and represented North America's democratization of the lawn. The philosophy was held by more than Frederick Law Olmsted; designers Andrew Jackson Downing and Frank J. Scott also believed lawns should be available to everyone, if only to look at. "It is unchristian to hedge from the sight of others the beauties of nature.... Throwing front grounds open together ... enriches all who take part in the exchange," wrote Scott in *The Art of Beautifying Suburban Home Grounds*, his 1870 treatise on landscape design. At the same time, the lawn provided a psychological line of demarcation from the street. As Kenneth Jackson says in his 1985 book *The Crabgrass Frontier: The Suburbanization of the United States*, "The lawn was a barrier, a kind of verdant moat separating the household from the threats and temptations of the city."

The Twentieth Century: The Recreational Influence

In the early twentieth century, golf, if you can believe it, moved the lawn ethic further along. So did North American cemeteries, which had also picked up on the idea of the grand park and were set on landscapes of sweeping grass. People both played and found eternal rest in the peace of a lawn.

The country's golf courses began modestly enough, three or four holes laid out in cow pastures or village greens, but the sport – and the properties on which it was played – grew like weeds after a rain. The Royal Montreal, the first permanent club in North America, was laid out in 1873 in Fletcher's Field, a cow pasture on Mount Royal in Montreal. By 1888, when St. Andrews (the oldest continuously operating club in the United States) was founded in another pasture in Yonkers, New York, Canada boasted six courses. By 1902, there were more than one thousand courses in the United States. Today the number

> "Let your lawn be your home's velvet robe, and your flowers its not too promiscuous decoration."
>
> Frank J. Scott

tops seventeen thousand in the United States and more than two thousand in Canada. Always a discriminating lot, golfers became more particular about the quality, thickness and height of the grasses they played on, and the new golf associations (the United States Golf Association [USGA] was formed in 1894; the Royal Canadian Golf Association [RCGA] in 1895) devoted many dollars to research and hybridization of new and improved grasses. With their sweeping vistas and immaculate lawns, golf courses became the great English parks of North America, available only to those who could afford to play the game.

As the continent grew up and entered the twentieth century, the garden club movement was born. The middle- to upper-class society matrons who ran these organizations spread the word about the desirability of a well-kept home and garden, and although they emphasized gardens more than lawns, they imprinted all who came their way with the need to keep up appearances. During the first half of the twentieth century, community and garden-club competitions became popular, and the new garden magazines encouraged readers to beautify their homes and neighborhoods with well-maintained landscaping. Children were involved in seed-growing competitions through Scouts, farm clubs and schools.

The Second World War was the turning point for the front lawn. After it was over the economy did more than return to normal – it boomed. Jobs were plentiful. Factories that had spent the previous decade turning out machines and materials for war were now making tons of consumer goods, and it was easy to convince a luxury-starved populace to buy them. There was a spanking white automatic washer and dryer for every laundry room and a shiny, chrome-laden car in every driveway. Big families were the norm, and a three-bedroom bungalow in the suburbs was affordable for the average family. The new housing developments that sprang up just outside the city limits boasted rows and rows of identical houses, and all those front yards needed grassing over. The lawn had finally made its way into the middle class.

The Birth of the Lawn Ethic

And all-important for the new democratic lawn was the means for growing ever-better grass. New power mowers were within the reach of every property owner. New pesticides and herbicides, originally developed for the killing fields of war, were now available at local garden centers, poised to annihilate every enemy of the perfect lawn. The war was over, times were good and people were settling down in a new world filled with families, peace and expanses of pristine green lawn.

The lawn became a given, a symbol of the good life, and a good lawn was proof of a properly lived life. All those children who'd grown up during the Depression and the Second World War learning (subliminally or otherwise) that a well-kept front lawn was another yardstick for measuring character, were ready to keep up with – or surpass – the Joneses. It was a marketing idea ripe for the picking, and manufacturers of the new power tools and the chemical companies eager to find a peacetime use for their wartime products were quick to promote the idea that you, too, could have a lawn as velvety and eternally green as any, as long as you bought their products.

Trouble was brewing, but it would take a few years for us to realize it.

"The lawn was one aspect of British culture that the Thirteen Colonies didn't reject when they proclaimed themselves a nation in 1776. In fact, they embraced the lawn with an enthusiasm that made England's lawn-love seem tame."

Robert Fulford

Planned Communities, Planned Lawns

Levittown, built on flat potato fields on Long Island, New York, was one of the first "planned communities" (as developers liked to call suburban housing developments) to be built in North America after the Second World War, and it became famous for founder Alexander Levitt's modern approach to organized living. He laid down rules for his suburbanites just as Frederick Olmsted (whose urban planning style set the trend nearly a century earlier) had done before him. Fences were not allowed, and lawns and weeds had to be cut and removed at least once a week between April 15 and November 15.

In 1951 E.P. Taylor began Canada's first planned community in a suburb of Toronto; called Don Mills, it was designed with curving streets and small, ranch-style houses. Applewood Acres, built on an orchard in what is now Mississauga, Ontario, by G.S. Shipp & Son, came hard on the heels of Don Mills: its little Monopoly houses on large lots went on the market on Mother's Day weekend in 1952, and 104 were sold in six days. Each house was sodded in the front and had at least one old apple tree per lot, plus a beautification bonus provided by the builder: a foundation planting of six shrubs. (One of these houses is now mine.) Residents of neither of these Canadian communities were told how to care for their lawns, but it was nevertheless understood that well-kept grass in the front yard was the rule.

Chapter Two

Lawn at What Cost?

Esthetics may have been the primary reason I finally dug up the lawn and planted a front yard garden, but I did have other more lofty considerations. Over the years I'd

come to consider our lawn more than merely boring: there seemed to be something wrong with it. The birds and the bees shunned it, the bugs stayed away in droves. There was no movement, no rustling, no chirping Jiminy crickets to leap up in front of me as I passed by on the pathway. Even on sunny days in a cool spring the cats ignored it, preferring to snooze in the earth of the perennial bed in the back, or to crouch, waggle and pounce in the shrubbery, fulfilling their destiny as the great African hunters of our neighborhood. As for me, walking around the corner of the house from the busy back garden to the barren front was like entering Rachel Carson's *Silent Spring*.

This was the mid-eighties, and in the twenty years since the publication of her book I had come a long way in my awareness of what human beings were doing to the planet. Carson had warned us in 1962 that the pesticides and herbicides, fungicides and rodenticides we'd been using in agriculture and home gardens since the Second World War were threats to all creatures who lived on or in the earth, not just the ones we were trying to get rid of.

Few paid heed to her message, and those who did were considered revolutionaries. Most of the public – and that included me – looked upon the new "environmentalists" as fanatics. I was part of the prevailing kill-'em-dead school of gardening, as advocated by my thick, all-purpose gardening book, a typical canon of the time. It spoke highly of new postwar chemicals for getting rid of interlopers, treat-

ing DDT, 2,4-D, chlordane and Lindane as the wonder drugs of the garden. It didn't overlook the old faithfuls, either, recommending lead arsenate at the rate of 15 pounds per 1000 square feet of lawn to control earthworms. The editors admitted grudgingly that our precious friends (as I eventually regarded them) the earthworms were "helpful to soils" but said they were "unsightly ... and make the surface bumpy and rough," strongly implying that lawns were better off without them.

And *this* was my bible.

In *Silent Spring* Carson wrote that we found ourselves in need of these poisonous elements in agriculture because we grew great fields of single crops, like corn and wheat, instead of using farming methods closer to natural ecosystems, such as crop rotation and smaller fields of mixed crops.

In other words, we liked monocultures. The problem with a monoculture is that it discourages visits from insects and animals that can't benefit in some way from the one kind of plant it contains, while attracting those who like to eat it. So you have large numbers of one or two species taking up residence at the feast, and soon find it necessary to bring out an arsenal of pesticides to kill them off. This is how the cycle begins.

Lawns are essentially monocultures containing a few species of turfgrass. Admittedly they're small monocultures compared to corn and wheat fields, but they add up. If I multiply the roughly 65-by-40-foot front lawns in my suburban neighborhood by the approximately 1,200 houses it contains, I arrive at 3,120,000 square feet. My neighborhood is bounded by another of similar size, and it in turn is adjacent to another, and then another, reaching all the way across the continent. This is a sweeping statement, but you get the picture. North Americans have about 24 million acres devoted to cultivated lawns, not including public parks, highway cloverleafs and embankments, cemeteries and golf courses. That's a lot of monoculture.

After years of gardening – and as I grew older and a little wiser – I began to really listen to the message of the environmentalists. The razing of woodlots and the loss of farmland for factories and monster housing developments in my growing city helped me understand how cavalierly we were treating our world, and how endangered the species in it were becoming. It seemed strange to send money to preserve the disappearing wildlife in the rainforests of the Amazon, or to sign petitions to save our own declining prairies, when we weren't considering the importance of nature in our own back (and front) yards.

The Impoverished Ecosystem

In many ways since we settled this continent we've altered and impoverished its ecosystems. We've built farms and villages and cities, gradually reducing to remnants the evergreen and deciduous forests of the north, east and west, the grasslands of the interior, and the deserts of the southwest. Given the amount of immigration this continent has experienced in a few short centuries, change like this is inevitable, if regretful. Still, while many of us mourn the loss of our natural heritage of forests and prairies, most of us insist on growing lawns of grasses native to the moist, cool conditions of England. We don't think of growing our own native grasses, the more beautiful but much taller little bluestem, or the drought-resistant and low-growing buffalo grass, because they don't fit with the prevailing fashion of clipped and cultivated lawns.

The smooth green lawn that so many North Americans aspire to is in fact an impoverished ecosystem. Think of your lawn as a large family of closely packed plants, growing together as a mat or a green carpet to beautify your front yard. But mat is probably the better word because the roots are encouraged to grow together in a tangle – the tighter the tangle, the more dense and thick the lawn. You water and feed your family of plants frequently to keep the roots from starving, then you trim off their tops before they can go to seed, which is, when it comes down to it, their biological destiny. So the crowded plants continue to grow frantically, fighting for air and food, trying madly to reproduce. Or at

The Greedy Golf Course

Golf courses, even environmentally friendly ones, are water hogs. They also like good feedings of fertilizer and beauty treatments of pesticides. Here's what a typical course receives in a year. Figures are in Canadian dollars.

- an inch of water a day during the golf season, about 125,000 gallons
- $22,000 worth of nitrogen fertilizer
- $2,400 worth of herbicides
- $2,300 worth of insecticides
- $11,900 worth of fungicides

least to take a nap, which they normally do in the heat of mid-summer, when most grasses fade to pale buff as they experience a natural dormant period. But the poor grass plants – all their efforts are to no avail because you keep feeding and watering them to keep them "healthy."

Your little family is sadly dysfunctional, but it will survive because of the attention you give it. A natural, working ecosystem – such as a forest, woodland or prairie – doesn't need so much human intervention. It operates on its own, powered almost entirely by the sun, which provides energy for photosynthesis and drives the water cycle. The plants in a healthy ecosystem have adapted to the location and the nutrients circulate successfully between them and the other residents – the birds, insects, even the soil. Plants die, break down and add humus to the soil. The spider eats the fly who's after the hibiscus, and the ladybugs eat the aphids sucking the sap out of the honeysuckle, and so the cycle continues.

If we left our non-native lawns alone forever, do you know what would happen? They would die and the land would try to revert to the forest or prairie that once grew on our properties. It's an idea that would be unsuccessful in our time simply because we wouldn't let it happen. We like our lawns too much. Besides, it would take at least a century.

I can't last that long, so I vote for a modified approach that will take less time: let's reduce our demands for large expanses of perfect, non-native grass, and try mixed front gardens. Something the birds and bees and Mother Nature will love. Something we can create without the help of a dangerous chemical cocktail of fertilizers and pesticides – and too much water.

The Chemical Invasion

After the Second World War dragons took up residence in our gardens, breathing larger and larger gusts of fire. In fifty years the pesticides Rachel Carson warned about wreaked more damage than two hundred years of settlement.

Few may have listened to Carson in the early sixties, but by the early seventies more evidence had surfaced suggesting some of these garden beasts were not the miracles they'd promised to be. As the years passed, several were suspected of causing serious health hazards among humans, pets and wildlife. DDT, Lindane, chlordane, diazinon and several other chemicals were suspected of having deadly side effects, among humans as well as wildlife, including cancer, birth defects and brain damage. Many of these lethal pesticides were eventually banned for use in the garden and on vegetable crops in the United States and Canada, although some are still used for killing insects elsewhere. Despite our enlightenment over the last thirty years about the dangers of destroying our environment, it's taking a long time to get these products off the shelves and out of our gardens.

Perhaps it's no wonder we accepted the new miracle chemicals so willingly, so naively, in those postwar years. They filled garden center shelves and their "innocent" virtues were extolled by garden writers and lawn-care experts, as well as in advertisements from the products' manufacturers. Still, one wonders how we could have accepted the idea that chemicals developed to kill great stands of jungle foliage or disease-bearing insects, or to support germ warfare, might not damage children, pets and wildlife, even if the directions on the label *were* followed exactly? The general attitude seemed to be that if a product was available to the public with a simple warning (usually in small print) to use it carefully, it must be safe.

Aggressive advertising campaigns helped to persuade the somewhat gullible public to use these products. During and after the Second World War, advertising and editorial copy promoting garden products took an interesting turn: it glamorized the war between humans and nature and consistently used the words of war to describe the benefits of using pesticides. Perhaps it was a sign of the times – the war itself and North America's postwar fear of communism – as much as an illustration of man's historical need to conquer nature.

The man-conquers-nature analogy didn't disappear as the war faded from memory. In 1980, a nylon-line weed trimmer, was likened to a gun: "The trimmer can be operated from a standing position so you don't have to stoop to conquer" read the article, "Simply squeeze the trigger of this remarkable weapon...."

In the world of lawns, there's always another enemy. In the seventies and eighties it was thatch, the layer of dead roots and blades of grass that builds up at the base of a thick lawn and suffocates it, preventing water and oxygen from reaching the soil and the healthy roots below. Naturally, new equipment was needed to free the lawn of this scourge: special dethatching rakes, turf thinners and aerators, and many of them were heralded by more stirring war imagery. In the 1970s, the advertising catchline for the Thatch-O-Matic (a "vertical mower" designed to cut through grass and thatch) was: When You Must Fight Thatch, Fight to Win!

And so gardeners fought the good fight against the enemies in their lawns – the earthworms, dew worms, Japanese beetles, slugs, snails, ants, chiggers, cutworms and so on. Homeowners took up arms against weeds, too, ignoring simple infantry tactics, like getting down on their hands and knees to dig up the dandelions one by one, to adopt wholesale slaughter with chemical warfare. Sometimes, if the label's directions were not assiduously followed, they managed to kill the nearby prize rhododendron as well.

Making Responsible Decisions

The companies who make pesticides say no study proves their products are dangerous to humans, and they have a point: a chemical that causes cancer in animals under selected laboratory conditions may not have the same effects on people who use pesticides in homes and on farms.

Still, there are plenty of studies out there that indicate some degree of connection between pesticides and toxic side effects in humans, and also raise the question of cumulative effects, poisoned air and groundwater runoff. "The world I work in is not black and white, there are many shades of gray," says Dr. Len Ritter, a professor in the department of environmental biology at the University of Guelph, Ontario. "You can find all kinds of papers arguing all sides of the question. To make your own decisions about using pesticides you have to weigh the totality of evidence, just as you'd do when embarking on a program of medication."

Even DDT has a beneficial side. It has been banned in the United States and Canada for years (see chart, opposite) because of its environmental persistence: it sticks around long after the bad bugs have been sprayed and kills good wildlife, too. "But it's probably saved more lives in Third World countries [where it's still used] than antibiotics, simply because it kills disease-bearing insects," Ritter says.

Ritter has no advice either way for people concerned about exposure to pesticides, except to advise they use them according to label instructions. "The average person who uses a pesticide properly a couple of times a season for ten minutes or so isn't likely going to be affected by it," he says. "The ones I worry about are the guys in the pest control industry, who could be working with these compounds for hours every working day. They could really get in trouble."

Nevertheless, we are gradually becoming more concerned about the dangers of the indiscriminate application of pesticides by homeowners and lawn-care companies. Many communities are withdrawing support for the cosmetic use of these products to keep private lawns, golf courses, parks and other public places green and weed-free all season. The little community of Hudson, Quebec, just outside Montreal, was a trailblazer in the movement. In 1991, long before many communities were even aware of problems, it passed a total ban of insecticides, herbicides and fungicides (all fall under the general term pesticides). A year later the ban was softened to allow pesticide use on golf courses and farms, and later some domestic spraying was temporarily allowed during an invasion of chinch bugs.

A Sampling of Environmental Pesticides

Only some of the pesticides listed below are still in use, and many were never sold for domestic purposes. The side effects on humans have not been proven for some because testing has only been done on laboratory animals, but some studies suggest poisoning has occurred. Pesticides are seldom actively banned. Sometimes they're withdrawn from sale by the manufacturers, but more often their registration is not renewed when it expires. In the United States and Canada, independent government testing is not done, although products are tested by independent, accredited laboratories and careful evaluation is made of the results.

Chemical	Side Effects*	Registration Expired
Organo-chlorine Insecticides Organo-chlorine compounds were first produced in the 1930s and were developed as poisonous gases in the Second World War. Converted to use as insecticides after the war, they're dangerous because they build up in fatty tissues over time, affecting the nervous and reproductive systems. The lawn-care industry has not used these products for about thirty years.		
DDT	• toxic to fish, affects liver, nervous and reproductive systems, carcinogenic	• U.S. 1972, Canada 1989. Still used elsewhere.
Lindane	• seizures, brain damage, birth defects	• U.S. 1983, Canada 2004. Some use still allowed to kill insects on livestock, and in lumber and seed grains
Chlordane	• found to be a human carcinogen in 1978	• U.S. 1978, Canada mid-1980s. Registration for termite control expired in 1990.
Organo-phosphate Insecticides Developed in the 1930s, these were used as nerve gasses in the Second World War. They account for half of all insecticides used in North America. Long-term exposure has been reported to cause nervous system damage.		
parathion	• extremely hazardous. Nausea, dizziness, increased heart rate, respiratory paralysis and death; used in agriculture only.	• U.S. 2000, Canada 2003
diazinon	• brain and nervous system damage; common home product	• U.S. 2003, Canada 2004
dursban (also known as chlorpyrifos)	• affects brains of fetal rats; weakness, vomiting and diarrhea, especially in children	• U.S. 2001, Canada 2005. Now used for agriculture only, particularly apples and grapes.
malathion	• nausea, dizziness, confusion, respiratory paralysis and death at high exposure	• in use for mosquito and boll weevil control, some agriculture and ornamental plants. Under evalution in Canada.
Hormonal Herbicides This family of growth stimulants causes distorted growth; broad-leafed plants essentially grow themselves to death.		
2, 4-D	• linked to non-Hodgkins lymphoma, birth defects, lowered male fertility, liver and kidney dysfunction, immune system deficiencies	• Still in use in Canada and the U.S. but under evaluation for continued registration in domestic use.
Early Insecticides Chemicals developed for use in wartime and converted to domestic or agricultural requirements aren't the only dangerous chemicals that have been used for pesticide control. Many older insecticides and herbicides were not only as deadly, but gardeners and farmers used them indiscriminately because they weren't aware of their potential.		
lead arsenate	• linked to cancer, brain and organ damage, cardiovascular problems. Remains in soil for many years.	• U.S. 1988, Canada 1978
nicotine sulfate	• highly toxic, suspected carcinogen	• Registration expired
potassium cyanate	• a herbicide that converts to cyanide in the body	• Canada 1973

*Observed or suspected side effects on wildlife and humans

In 1993, however, despite Hudson's compromises, the ban was challenged by two lawn-care companies, Chemlawn and Spray-Tech, who felt they should be allowed to continue to do business with residents of the town. They took their arguments to the Quebec Supreme Court. They lost. The companies went to the Quebec Court of Appeals, and lost again. But they didn't give up: the case went to the Supreme Court of Canada, which ruled in June, 2001, that the town of Hudson did indeed have the jurisdiction to enact a bylaw to restrict the use of pesticides within municipal boundaries, including on private property. The ruling motivated many communities across Canada to seek similar bylaws and about fifty, including Toronto, Victoria and Halifax, have either enacted their own bylaws or are in the process of seeking bans on pesticide use for public and private lands.

Change: One Garden at a Time

But let's not demonize grass itself. Like all plants, it generates oxygen through photosynthesis – according to the Turfgrass Producers International, a U.S industry group, a 50-by-50-foot lawn produces enough oxygen to meet the needs of a family of four. A lawn has a cooling effect, it absorbs gaseous pollutants, it prevents soil erosion, filters contaminants from rainwater and reduces water runoff.

It's the way people grow grass that's the problem: in great swaths, creating monocultures that don't provide the biodiversity this world needs to survive. Most of us apply too much fertilizer, more than the roots can absorb, and it seeps down into the sewers, where it finds its way into nearby lakes and eventually our water supply. If we use pesticides we kill beneficial bugs and upset the balance of nature, to say nothing of possibly affecting our own health. Then we mow the grass down with huge power mowers that belch smoke and destroy the peace of a weekend morning, plus giving us something to choke on. In the view of critics of pampered lawns, most of this negates the lawn's original benefits.

In many places it is still the responsibility of the individual gardener to decide whether or not to use chemicals on the lawn and in the garden. For my part, I gave up wholesale pesticide spraying of my extensive flower garden early in my gardening years. I admit it wasn't because I knew something others didn't or I had a special concern for the environment. Messing around with pump sprayers was just too darn much trouble. But I soon realized that without pesticides ... nothing happened. I wasn't beset by a plague of locusts or a host of plant diseases. And that was the end of my association with pesticides.

My husband was much smarter about this than I was. He actually read the labels of the products he was using for the lawn (his territory; the gardens were mine), got a little suspicious about the oblique warnings, and decided a lawn service was better equipped than he to take the risks. Once he realized that dead grubs also meant dead earthworms and dead soil, he switched to an organic lawn service. By the early eighties I was converted. Years before I'd retired my 1950s chemical-friendly gardening book and bought a few up-to-date ones, which don't even mention DDT, chlordane or malathion. And I subscribed to an organic gardening magazine.

I made a compost heap in the back corner, and when plastic composters became available I bought two of them. I learned to live with bugs (except for tomato hornworms, which still terrify me). I planted bee balm, berry bushes and butterfly milkweed to attract wildlife to my garden. I planted a front garden. I realized I wanted to save the world. Then I realized I couldn't save the world, but I could change my own garden.

Then I thought that maybe, just maybe, my neighbors and all their friends might take up the cause. Maybe, just maybe, we could weave together a network of poison-free, biodiverse, nature-friendly gardens that would, in the end, make a difference.

And that has become my quest.

Nature, the Corporate Way

When employees at Husky Injection Molding Systems in Bolton, Ontario, look out their office windows they don't see parking lots, they see naturalized gardens. The cars are there, but they're cunningly hidden by wide islands of tamarack, spruce, maples, crab apples, Queen Anne's lace, mullein and asters. The wide beds around the modern corporate buildings are designed with stone pathways lined with casual shrubs such as witch hazel, dogwood and wayfaring tree, underplanted with black-eyed Susans, native grasses and thymes. The patio outside one cafeteria overlooks a jade green pond and waterfall; it's a holding pond for storm water, part of Husky's innovative water-management system.

At the entrances, the plantings are deliberately more colorful: yellow native grasses, deep violet verbena, purple heliotrope and pink chrysanthemums. It seems no wonder that in 1995 Husky received the Lieutenant Governor's Conservation Award for outstanding achievement in protecting Ontario's natural environment, and the Financial Post's gold award in environmental leadership in 1994.

Paul Ehnes of Greenery Unlimited, who plants and maintains the gardens, jokes that soil improvement is at the bottom of everything in the garden. He brings in leaf mold, pine bark and compost made from vegetable market leftovers, piles it on the soil of new beds and tills it in. Plants aren't watered, except by hand their first year, and weeds such as clover, dandelions and twitch grass are often allowed to stay because they provide mulch and prevent soil erosion. Pesticides and herbicides are never used, and the gardens sing with the sounds of birds and insects.

The Ideal Lawn: Don't Try This at Home

The lawn in front of Manulife Financial, a stately Georgian-style head office in the heart of Toronto, is so perfect passersby often have to touch it to make sure it's real grass. It's a uniform paint-box green, velvety smooth, meticulously manicured, totally weedless – and well used. Both the general public and employees of the company, a well-established provider of financial products and services, are encouraged to stroll on the grass, lie on it, eat lunch on it or otherwise enjoy it, although practice putts and football scrimmages are definitely discouraged.

The lawn has been a city landmark and a stop for tour buses almost since the embryo patch of creeping bent grass that started it all was transplanted to the grounds (from a local golf course) when the building was erected in 1925. It was a time when a beautiful corporate lawn was indeed a status symbol. Looking after it has always required time and money – today a staff of three full-time horticulturists and a summer student tend to it – but Manulife is dedicated to its upkeep because the green carpet of perfect grass has become a company trademark.

The lawn has been the baby of chief horticulturist Jeff McMann since 1991, and he greets sunrise every weekday morning, coffee and a magnifying glass in hand, to eyeball the turf for early signs of disease, raccoon damage, misplaced divots, doggie-doo or ridges from bicycle tires (the gates are left open in the evening to allow visitors to enter). Since Jeff has been in charge, environmentally friendly procedures have been the rule.

"Observation is the key to identifying needed repairs or potential problems," Jeff says. "For example, raccoons dig up turf if there are certain insects under it, and starlings are indicators of other kinds of bugs." Not that bugs would have much chance with Jeff and his co-workers on constant watch. He's also in regular contact with other Canadian and American caretakers of bent grass on golf courses and bowling greens, to be aware of bugs that might be heading his way. And Environment Canada's weekly weather forecast is invaluable because it not only helps plan watering schedules (sprinklers are programed to run from midnight to six a.m., depending on need), but alerts Jeff to conditions that could be favorable to certain turf diseases. "Healthy grass resists disease, and we need to keep ours in top shape," Jeff says.

Herbicides aren't used to kill weeds. "Some are actually detrimental in the long run, and we prefer to pull the weeds out as we cut the grass," Jeff says. "But bent grass grows tight, so it's hard for weeds to get established." In the years he's been in charge insecticides haven't been needed, probably because of the preventative measures taken. Fungicides are employed only when absolutely necessary.

The lawn is dethatched (scraped of a layer of accumulated dead cuttings) a couple of times a year and aerated (a process where holes are punched into the grass at intervals to allow air into the soil) two or three times a season. Fertilizer is applied about eight times a season, using half the required dose, and soil tests are done biannually to assess which fertilizers are required.

As for cutting the grass, that happens three to five times a week, depending on conditions, with push mowers. The mowers use a variety of patterns, just like suburbanites do – sometimes a checkerboard, sometimes a diagonal – so the blades don't bend one way. "We maintain a height of about five-sixteenths of an inch, depending on weather and time of year," says Jeff. "Bent grass grows faster than any other grass." After the lawn is cut, the keepers check the clippings to judge the sharpness of the cutting blades. Overseeding takes place in spring and fall, using the 'Penncross' and 'Pennlink' bent grass varieties developed by the University of Pennsylvania.

This is the kind of lawn grass aficionados would die for. "But you wouldn't want it," Jeff says. "Think of the maintenance."

Chapter Three

Evolution of a Garden

Like most epiphanies, my revelation about front yard gardens came to me in a flash, after years of simmering quietly in my subconscious. You might say it came to me in

the flesh, too, alive and blooming on a corner lot in Amsterdam, where I was on a garden tour in 1991. Until the moment I saw that garden I hadn't realized the depth of my desire to grow something more esthetically pleasing than grass in front of my house.

Front yard gardens seemed to be the norm in Amsterdam. On this tour I'd seen tiny formal ones of stone, statuary and shrubbery, and middle-sized ones planted with hundreds of yellow daffodils (it was Holland, after all). But this one struck a chord. It undulated with plants – spring bulbs of every hue, perennials pregnant with buds, rhododendrons, mounding mugo pines and nest spruce – all of which flowed continuously from the foundation of the house to the roadside. Something about the house reminded me of my own: it was small and made of brick – although painted white, unlike mine – and it had a gently sloping lot with one tree, bare at the moment, as was my apple tree back home. When I saw the garden I almost shouted "Eureka!"

It was more than this dwelling's resonance with my own little house that suddenly made me realize how much I wanted a front garden. The timing was right. For years I'd been an unquestioning gardener who accepted the unwritten rule of the lawn, experimenting with garden styles in my backyard and leaving the grass for my neighbors to approve of and my husband to mow. Our suburban neighborhood was grass as far as the eye could see, although

Above: I came home from Holland to a nice-enough front yard. Our small Monopoly house had undergone a main-floor renovation and facade facelift, and we added new, wider steps and a curved flagstone pathway, plus refurbished and enlarged foundation plantings. But there was too much grass for my taste. My Holland trip had planted in my mind the seed of a front yard garden, and I had plans. Opposite: My front yard garden, ten years later.

most front yards also boasted an ancient apple tree, courtesy of a contractor who managed to preserve the orchard on which he built his postwar subdivision. We also had the requisite foundation planting under the picture window and a columnar evergreen at each corner of the house, all of them overgrown and awkward.

I found our front lawn more than a little boring, but I was busy in the back trying a meadow, then a pink garden, then a white one, á la Vita Sackville-West's much-copied garden at Sissinghurst. I'd been gardening since the fifties, but was still a slave to trends. No matter what garden style I was developing, and then tearing out because it didn't work the way the books said it would, I loved the atmosphere in the backyard. The overflowing beds had taken over almost the whole space and were visited by bees, good and bad bugs, lovely butterflies and birds, great numbers of pesky squirrels, the occasional shy fox at dawn and dusk, and the neighborhood cats, who seemed to consider my garden their personal jungle.

When I walked around to the front, the atmosphere changed: no bugs, no birds, no butterflies, no animals. Worse, no personality. My back garden was not only a natural beauty, it was nature friendly, offering diversity in plants and insects and other garden guests – some less welcome than others, I admit. The no-man's land of barren grass stretching from the house to the road in the front, edged with sad shrubs, a concrete sidewalk and a big, black asphalt driveway, was in serious need of help, at least in my view. It needed new and more diverse plants, as well as a general facelift. To add another dimension to the challenge, I was running out of space in the back for my garden maneuvers.

Nature was alive and well in my back garden. After the light went on in my brain on my visit to Amsterdam, I resolved it would reside in the front, too.

My inspiration: the sweet, flower-filled Dutch garden I saw on a tour of Holland a dozen years ago sent me home on a mission to have my own front garden.

Stage One: Starting Small

Like most men I know, my husband had always liked cutting the front lawn – I swear it's a guy thing. One week he'd run the mower from the front of the house to the road, the next he'd cut crosswise, from the driveway to the neighbor's lot line. The third week he'd go corner to corner. He liked the roar of the power mower – maybe he was even hooked on the gas fumes – and the challenge of cutting the grass in the ditch without shaving it clean on the steepest part of the slope. He commented many times that he did his best thinking while mowing the lawn.

So you can see that my husband was the first hurdle in developing my plan for a front yard garden. My own creativity was also a problem: I had no books to consult, no models to follow, save for my Amsterdam inspiration, and frankly I didn't know where to begin.

Luckily, we'd just completed a ground floor and facade renovation, so it seemed obvious to begin at the house. We were going to have to replace the old concrete-slab front walk, which had been damaged by the contractor's equipment. The grass had been chewed up, too, and the overgrown foundation planting looked distinctly uncomfortable against the new windows. The concrete steps to the door (like the walk, they dated back to when the house was built in the fifties) were narrow and relatively steep, and the front stoop so small it barely held two people. If we opened the door on three, one of our guests was likely to be tossed into the shrubbery.

With the help of a garden designer we installed a curving path of flagstones set in pea gravel that swept from the driveway to wide, shallow stone steps leading up to a generous stone entrance pad. Past the steps, the pathway bulged into a small sitting area, then disappeared around the side of the house into the back garden. The stonework looked lovely, and the new, more gracious entranceway welcomed all who approached the house. But it cried out for a similarly graceful foundation planting. The designer

The first step toward a complete front garden was to persuade my husband, who claimed he did his best thinking while cutting the grass, that we could do with a little less lawn. Once I'd won him over, I hired a couple of out-of-work teenagers for the backbreaking job of removing the grass for a sweeping bed beside the driveway.

Stage Two: The Move is On

The next year I filled in the spaces around the new foundation plantings with annuals and planted dozens of spring-flowering bulbs. But I still wasn't satisfied with the look, and I began to eye the grass on the other side of the pathway.

But I moved carefully. A couple of summers later I mentioned to my husband casually that there was still a lot of grass for him to look after (our frontage is 65 feet, and the depth from roadside to house is about 35 feet), considering that his real weekend avocation was playing touch football. I also commented as subtly as I could that the demarcation line between the new path and the grass seemed rather stark, and I thought it would benefit by a border garden to soften the look.

Well, okay, he said after a bit of mulling, no doubt noting my unexpectedly positive comment about touch football, as long as I left a good portion of grass to suit the neighbors and himself. But who would dig the new border? His back wouldn't take it.

Leave it to me, I said. Luckily there were a few unemployed teenagers around who needed work. We started in late summer and they toiled ceaselessly while I supervised, using the yellow extension cord I'd laid down as a digging guideline to mark the boundary. They lifted the turf, dug trenches about eight inches deep and put the turf upside down in the bottom. Then they replaced the soil. I'm sure they thought I was crazy, but they had strong backs. The grass eventually decayed and added nutrients to the soil and, except for the odd stray blade, it has never reappeared.

The border was wide and shaped vaguely like a "C," extending in one swoop from partway across the frontage at the road, narrowing a bit as it followed the driveway, and widening again across the front of the house. Before it was completely dug the first problem arose: a city inspector dropped a note in our mailbox to say we couldn't plant in the ditch or we'd impede the flow of storm water. Humbug: there was a house around the corner with a full ditch garden

suggested raising the beds three feet higher than ground level (a wooden well was built around one small basement window to hold back the soil), and sloping the beds gradually downward to the pathway, creating wide foundation plantings with no grass between path and house.

No grass! I couldn't believe my ears! I couldn't have asked for a more auspicious suggestion. With judicious pruning we managed to save a number of the evergreens and, to keep things low, we added new dwarf varieties and spreading ground covers that eventually spilled out over the flagstone and hid the boundaries between path and plantings.

It was a painless beginning, and my husband loved it.

that had been there for years. Had a suspicious neighbor complained? I decided to keep a low profile and dutifully resodded part of the ditch.

I knew the garden literally had to keep a low profile, otherwise it would have too much prominence on our street of lawns. The soil was sandy and the lot faced west, with a slight slope down to the road – in hot summers it could be desert-like. Near the road I had in mind a "tapestry" of creeping thymes; this expression had caught my fancy in a garden book, suggesting interlacing plants so close together they allowed no ground to show. So in went various varieties of thymes, plus other low mounding plants like false rock cress, bellflower (a pretty thing with starry flowers, and as rampant as they come: it's now taken over the ditch, but the bylaw officer hasn't noticed), moss phlox and evergreen candytuft. To keep the soil from washing down into the ditch I embedded flat stones horizontally into the slope; now they're almost covered by the trailing plants. For winter interest I planted a creeping juniper, and now it's almost invisible in summer, overgrown by the perennial plants.

On the driveway side, the low mounders were joined by creeping baby's breath, rock rose and the accommodating bergenia, which likes both sun and shade and tolerates dry or moist soils. I massed several bergenia under the apple tree, and planted a sweet autumn clematis to ramp up its branches, for its white froth of bloom.

These plants were essentially chosen because they were low, although I also stuck to a palette of blues, purple-to-lavender and shades of pink. Like most gardeners I made a list of the plants that met my needs before I went to the nursery, and then impulsively bought more. Mistakes were made: one "coral" rock rose bloomed glaring orange, and it does to this day, but it's such a prolific bloomer I can't bear to take it out.

For the section alongside the new gravel and flagstone path at the top of the "C," however, I did adhere to a planting plan. For this section I'd decided on varieties that grew a little taller: a wide ribbon of blue catmint bordered with

Within a couple of years the driveway garden was filling in with expanding patches of moss phlox (*Phlox subulata*), rock cress (*Aubrieta*), daffodils (*Narcissus*) and grape hyacinth (*Muscari*) in spring, with transplanted perennials and volunteer annuals the rest of the season. Even our cat, Madame Mao, learned that a variety of plants had more hunting and exploring potential than grass.

chartreuse lady's mantle and cushion spurge, accented with furry gray lamb's ears. I borrowed this idea from another book, and it worked beautifully.

For the sake of my budget, only some of these plants were purchased the first fall; the rest had to wait until the following spring. This turned out to be good timing for more than one reason: in late October, a couple of weeks after I'd put in about five hundred spring-blooming bulbs on the driveway side, the waterworks department knocked on our door. Hadn't we been told they'd be digging up part of our lot to put in larger water pipes? they asked incredulously. This time I didn't keep a low profile.

The alarmed workmen skimmed off the first few inches of earth so I could retrieve the bulbs. They treated me like I was an artery about to burst. Then the city reimbursed me a

A sturdy arbor was designed to visually extend the width of our small house and welcome visitors into the back garden under a dense Japanese wisteria (*Wisteria floribunda*). In spring, the wisteria is complemented by our neighbor's honeysuckle (*Lonicera*).

hundred bucks for plants and bulbs that were lost or damaged in the digging.

I'd learned the lesson of the squeaky wheel.

Stage Three:
Invasion of the Grass Snatchers

Another couple of years passed, the plants filled in and were discovered by the bees and butterflies from the back garden. Volunteers showed up, in particular a band of fluffy pink annual poppies; they were too tall for my low-profile plantings but so wantonly showy they soon became the stars of the July garden. They were, I learned, opium poppies, probably illegal. No poppy police showed up so I let them stay, but made them behave – they seed themselves recklessly, and if left to their own devices will choke out everything in a garden. (Another warning: they look lovely while in bloom, but the foliage soon withers and leaves ugly brown remnants while the attractive seed pods form.)

Other surprises appeared, such as common yellow mullein, which obviously decided it liked our garden better than its native roadside, and snow-in-summer, which I'm sure snuck in with a friend's offering of plants. The single five-foot mullein added a dramatic exclamation point to the garden and a surprising color note. Unfortunately, it's a biennial and didn't last past its second year. The unwelcome and invasive snow-in-summer I'm still trying to eradicate. But such is the way of a garden. The garden grew so well I couldn't believe it – it was as if the soil had been waiting for plants other than grass to inhabit it. Soon it came to the point where it was taking care of itself, requiring little more than some editing spring and fall to keep plants under control. I was itching to take up the rest of the grass and complete my dream garden, but I needed a plan. I worked on several, but as always they failed because I could envision perfection better in my mind's eye than on paper. I confess the plan remained in my head to the end – I've never been a Gertrude Jekyll, who was known for her beautifully color-balanced, meticulous planting plans.

Of course I needed my husband's okay for the full monty – to say nothing of his help. But he was turning out to be a hard sell. He was loath to give up his Saturday morning power outings, however brief they were before touch football practice took over. He thought our small patch of green in the front looked just fine, and what would the neighbors say? Besides, when would we have the time to look after more garden? I bided my time, knowing he'd eventually come around.

Fate intervened in the form of an infestation of white grubs. The little beasts ate half our patch of green, leaving it sad and brown. We called in our former lawn-care company (which had converted from chemicals to organic methods) and the nice young man took one look and reluctantly said the only way he could get rid of the grubs was to spray with diazinon. Of course, it would also kill the earthworms, plus every other small being that resided in the soil.

And would diazinon keep the grubs away? Well, maybe not. They'd been on the march from regions south of us for some time, and the year before had turned the corner of our street and discovered a huge buffet of grass. "We'll eat like kings!" I'm sure I'd heard them exclaim as they settled down to devour the neighborhood lawns.

"Okay, the grass goes and the garden's in," said my husband at the mention of diazinon. "As long as I don't have to dig it up." (He was already seeing his chiropractor nearly every month.)

And so I was catapulted into the final stage of the garden – if a garden can ever be said to have a final stage. My plans weren't completely formulated, but *carpe diem*.

As the years passed and the driveway border filled in, with volunteers like an annual poppy (*Papaver somniferum*) and oxeye daisy (*Leucanthemum vulgare*) appearing randomly, I yearned to take over the rest of the grass. But it was a hard sell. Luck was with me in the form of white grubs, who descended on our neighborhood and left our lawn patchy and brown. Thus began the next stage: the full monty. Soon I was hiring more help to dig up the remaining lawn.

Stage Four: The Final Frontier

We hired another nice young man to remove the grass, but he was past his teen years and not so willing to dig trenches and bury the sod upside down. Instead, he skimmed it off with a sod cutter and trucked it away. I can still see all that wonderful compost driving off down the street.

With the grass gone, I had my first opportunity to see the yard as a whole and plan the finished garden. A moment of panic ensued. I stood on the road and then on the front steps and did some creative squinting. This revealed that the garden would need a couple of paths, to provide structure and access to the plants, and for the post-man, who quickened his pulse every morning by leaping over the flower border on his way to the lawn and the house next door. I dragged out the yellow extension cord again, pulled out all the hoses I could find, and laid them out as pathway boundaries. Then I walked down the street away from the garden, did an about-face and recorded my immediate impressions. This simple technique eventually helped me to place the pathways so they looked graceful as well as fulfilling their purpose.

As I pondered the pathways the days went by and the neighbors began to wonder. One asked if we were planning to put in sod or to seed the new lawn. I said, well, neither, I had a new plan in the works. After a couple of days she returned to ask if I needed help. The woman next to me also politely enquired as to my plans. Dirt in the front yard obviously didn't meet neighborhood standards. So I started talking, describing to my neighbors what I was planning

and why. They began to look interested, if skeptical. When one of my next door neighbors suggested our sunny front yard would be a great spot for a few tomato plants and some herbs, I knew I'd won her over.

Once I had decided on the position of the pathways, my husband and I spent a weekend putting them in. It was simple: we dug shallow trenches two feet wide and four inches deep. Landscape fabric, a woven material used to block out weeds, was laid in the trench and limestone screenings were poured in up to soil level. Voila.

The garden itself took a little longer, but I took some shortcuts. I knew I had neither the back nor the time to improve the soil – and why did the whole area need amending anyway, despite our thin, sandy soil? I decided to take a personalized approach: as I planted, I'd dig a good-sized hole for each plant and mix in compost and slow-release fertilizer with the excavated soil before it was replaced.

And so it was down to business. One of our priorities was wind and sound protection at the southwest corner of our lot, where the noise of a nearby highway sometimes swept in. I started there, grouping a couple of red osier dogwoods and lime green double Japanese kerria, whose branches provide dramatic winter color although their summer looks leave something to be desired. (I'm not doing the kerria justice – its bright gold, fully double blossoms are delightful in spring). I also put in a budget-pleaser: a couple of lovely plants their donor, a fellow gardener, says are a variety of euonymus, with glossy evergreen foliage and dark purple berries in fall. Nearer the house, a fragrant Carolina spice bush joined the group, as did a bright candy pink rhododendron I fell for at the nursery because it was in full, radiant bloom on a dull spring day. One should know better.

In the middle of the garden I planted an Eastern redbud because I had to have one, even though it cost the groceries for a month. It's strikingly beautiful in spring, with pink flowers creeping along the branches, and its heart-shaped leaves are a yummy light green in summer and bright yellow in fall.

The garden took off, and within a few years was so full it needed frequent thinning. In spring, opposite and above, grape hyacinths (*Muscari*), catmint (*Nepeta mussinii*) and lady's mantle (*Alchemilla mollis*), bordering path, contrast with chartreuse cushion spurge (*Euphorbia polychroma*). Rose-flowered bergenia (*Bergenia cordifolia*) and prairie smoke (*Geum triflorum*), near the garden light, opposite, add to the show. In summer, below, the plantings by the path near the willow arbor change to pinks, blues and white.

In spring the redbud tree (*Cercis canadensis*) branches out in glorious pink, above. Mauve moss phlox (*Phlox subulata*) and 'Lilac Wonder' species tulip (*Tulipa bakeri* 'Lilac Wonder'), below, show their pretty faces.

These were the big expenses the first year, plus a few perennials to form the basic planting. I filled with annuals and moved plants from the back garden. In the years since, I moved lavender that wasn't doing well there because of increasing shade, and five 'The Fairy' roses that had outgrown their place. The roses I placed in an arc that follows one branch of the front pathway, and they bloom their heads off from July to October. Some annuals, such as Clary sage and bright yellow California poppies, planted as seeds the first year, come up in different places every summer, and Joe-Pye weed, a perennial native and a complete stranger to my garden, decided to take up residence in the ditch. Joe is one of the few plants I've taken out: he was too tall for the generally low growth of the garden.

Our beloved old apple tree blew over one windy fall night, still bearing a few apples, and the sweet autumn clematis died with it. In the apple tree's place I planted a purple smoke tree, a shrub with brilliant purple foliage and deep pink inflorescences (flowers sprays), in early summer.

Many of our neighbors are still battling white grubs, replacing patches of grass every year, but although I always find a few grubs when I dig in the garden, they look thin and undernourished. The roots of my plants are too far apart for them to dine well. More of our neighbors are taking up the garden cause, however. The second year my tomato-loving neighbor extended the postman path (which ended at the property line between our houses) around to her front door. Then she planted a raised bed of dogwood and ornamental grasses on one side of the path and a big bed of hostas on the other. The neighbor on the other side dug up part of her grass in a wide curving bed and laid down gravel dotted with some evergreens. The young man who lives across the road has dug up the part of his front lawn eaten by white grubs and made a garden of yellow daylilies and ornamental grasses. He jokes that its shape is like a map of Italy, and he's not far wrong.

A couple of summers ago we replaced the ugly asphalt driveway with random cobblestones; it carries the cottage look of our house and garden even further. The

Garden Plan

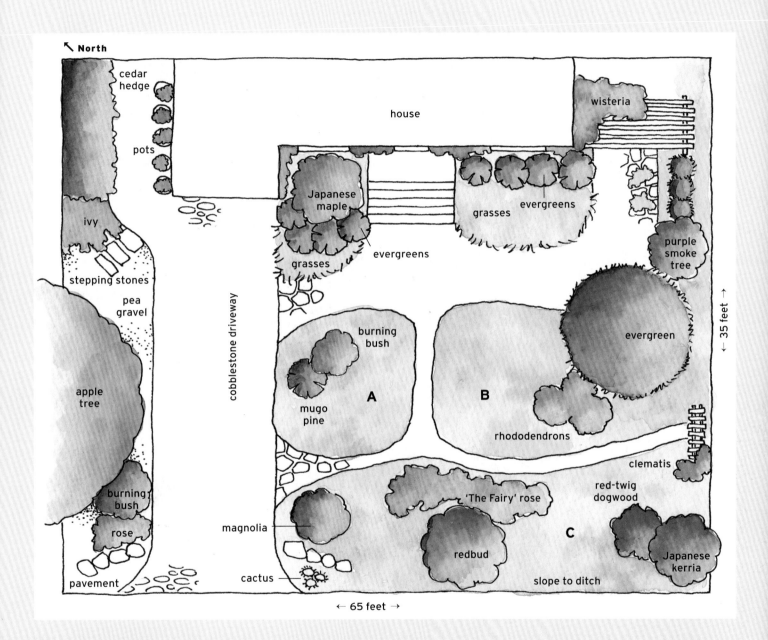

North

cedar hedge

pots

ivy

stepping stones

pea gravel

apple tree

burning bush

rose

pavement

house

wisteria

Japanese maple

evergreens

grasses

evergreens

grasses

purple smoke tree

cobblestone driveway

burning bush

mugo pine

A

B

evergreen

rhododendrons

clematis

red-twig dogwood

magnolia

'The Fairy' rose

C

cactus

redbud

Japanese kerria

slope to ditch

← 35 feet →

← 65 feet →

A catmint, lamb's ears, cushion spurge, lady's mantle, prairie smoke, bergenia, rock rose, creeping baby's breath, mullein, blue fescue, rock cress

B catmint, lady's mantle, cushion spurge, butterfly bush, yucca, bugleweed, columbine, Russian sage, veronica, allium, mallow, heather

C 'Blue Clips' campanula, lavender, purple coneflower, shasta daisies, thyme, moss phlox, pasqueflower, lilies, gaura, cupid's dart, fern-leaf bleeding heart, aubrietia

All beds heavily planted with spring bulbs and self-seeding annuals: California poppy, opium poppy, oxeye daisies, mullein, Clary sage

same summer I found a place for yet another garden: I dug up the grass on the far side of the driveway adjoining my neighbor's gravel beds, and created a scree garden of gravel and larger stones. Here it's hot and dry, so I've planted a patch of native cacti and some ground-cover roses near the ditch to please people who walk by, who invariably stop to chat when I'm out in the garden.

My husband often comments how much less work the garden is than the lawn was, and he's right, partly because the garden is mostly my domain. But after the spring weeding (of which he does half), thinning and editing, it pretty much survives all summer on its own, except for necessary irrigation during dry spells.

And as for satisfying his obsession with grass, well, he's been forced to take up golf.

Sometimes a jarring note like the orange tulip in this photo creeps in, but it can be justified by its relative proximity to the chartreuse cushion spurge (*Euphorbia polychroma*). The crimson-flashed single late tulip 'Arctic Flame' has a dramatic presence, and echo white tulips scattered through the garden. Under the redbud: the shiny spring foliage of 'The Fairy' rose.

Plants

Spring

bellflower (*Campanula rapunculoides*)

candytuft (*Iberis sempervirens*)

crocus (*Crocus*)

cushion spurge (*Euphorbia polychroma*)

daffodil (*Narcissus*)

double kerria (*Kerria japonica* 'Pleniflora')

dwarf bearded iris (*Iris* x *Pumila*)

Eastern redbud (*Cercis canadensis*)

fern-leaf bleeding heart (*Dicentra formosa* 'Luxuriant')

'Manchu Fan' magnolia (*Magnolia* 'Manchu Fan')

moss phlox (*Phlox subulata*)

prairie smoke (*Geum triflorum*)

rhododendrons (*Rhododendron* PJM 'Olga Mezitt' and 'Ramapo')

rock cress (*Aubrieta*)

rock rose (*Helianthemum*)

tulips (early to late)

Summer to Late Summer

'Blue Clips' bellflower (*Campanula carpatica* 'Blue Clips')

butterfly bush (*Buddleia davidii* 'Dubonnet')

creeping baby's breath (*Gypsophila repens*)

cupid's dart (*Catananche caerulea*)

English lavender (*Lavandula angustifolia* 'Munstead' and 'Hidcote')

'The Fairy' rose (*Rosa* 'The Fairy')

gauras (*Gaura lindheimeri* 'Siskiyou Pink' and 'Whirling Butterflies')

lady's mantle (*Alchemilla mollis*)

plumbago (*Ceratostigma plumbaginoides*)

Russian sage (*Perovskia atriplicifolia*)

'Six Hills Giant' catmint (*Nepeta faassenii* 'Six Hills Giant')

Fall Color

burning bush (*Euonymus alatus*)

'Clara Curtis' chrysanthemum (*Chrysanthemum* x *rubellum* 'Clara Curtis')

colchicums (*Colchicum* 'Waterlily' and 'The Giant')

'Purple Dome' aster (*Aster novae-angliae* 'Purple Dome')

Foliage Plants and Shrubs

blue fescue (*Festuca glauca*)

blue rug creeping juniper (*Juniperus horizontalis* 'Wiltonii')

'Bressingham Ruby' bergenia (*Bergenia* 'Bressingham Ruby')

Carolina spice bush (*Calycanthus floridus*)

lamb's ears (*Stachys byzantina*)

purple smoke tree (*Cotinus coggygria* 'Royal Purple')

red osier dogwood (*Cornus sericea*)

sweet autumn clematis (*Clematis terniflora*)

thymes

Self-Seeding Annuals

California poppy (*Eschscholzia californica*)

catchfly (*Silene*)

Clary sage (*Salvia viridis* syn. *S. horminum*)

opium poppy (*Papaver somniferum*)

Rhododendron

California poppy, blue rug creeping juniper, and 'Blue Clips' bellflower

Chapter Four

Groundwork

Now that you've been inspired to get rid of the grass and plant a front yard garden, where do you begin? This is the gardener's dilemma. We may have pictures in our

minds of what we'd like, but we have no idea how to transport them into our own space, let alone turn our garden into an oasis of beauty that stops people in their tracks as they walk down the street.

And here is the main difference between gardening in the front and gardening in the back: the neighbors can see it, and that can be intimidating. You can make all the mistakes you like in the back and no one will know but your nearest and dearest. But in the front! Everyone can view your inexperience, your lack of artistic ability and your questionable garden housekeeping. Horrors! That can be daunting.

On the other hand, you really shouldn't worry. Nature is wonderful, and manages to weave plants together in a pleasing mass even if there isn't much of a planting plan (my own garden is a good example). You just have to look at fields, meadows and plantings along rail lines to see how nature works her magic. Things *fit*. If you want a plant-focused front garden, take a lesson from nature. In most cases, the secret is to stay loose.

But the plantings are the last thing you have to worry about ... first you have to decide on the type of garden you want. Should it be a cottage-style garden? An enclosed courtyard? Something formal? Something wild? Maybe you're feeling tentative, and just want to put your toe in the cold water of front yard gardens to see if you like it. Perhaps your property is a postage stamp and you don't think you can

Consulting professionals with the equipment and expertise to improve drainage, install paths or nudge boulders into place is a good first step if you have a particular design challenge. Suzanne Scott's plain front yard (above) sloped from the street to the house, creating runoff into her neighbor's drive. By installing a rockery with variegated hostas and rhododendrons with weeping tiles buried underneath, the Scotts eliminated the overflow and now have a beautiful garden view from their front porch (opposite).

do much with it (take heart – tiny gardens are the easiest to design). Whatever your situation, the ideas presented by the gardeners in the following chapters will keep you up nights dreaming up different plans for your own front garden.

Perhaps you have a site problem, like the gardener in this chapter, who was aware of a drainage difficulty but unsure of how serious it was or how to deal with it. If you suspect a problem of some kind, don't ignore it. Get professional advice. Believe me, it's a good investment.

Getting a pro to help you design your garden is a good investment even if you don't have a problem but aren't really sure what you want. Find a good garden designer or landscape architect through your city's landscape architect association, ads in magazines or the recommendations of friends. Ask to see some of their work, and don't be shy about rejecting one whose style doesn't fit with your own. Usually the initial consultation is free. A good designer will ask lots of questions about what you like and come up with at least a couple of alternative plans. If you have a limited amount of money, ask in advance for a price for the plan, and ask to have it designed as phased-in plantings so you can accomplish it yourself at your own speed – and within your budget. If you've got the world to spend, of course you can have the designer find a contractor and have the whole job installed the first year. But that will be less fun.

The common-sense, fairly basic advice in this chapter is meant to help gardeners who've been inspired to create their own gardens, and much of it is implicit in the profiles of garden styles that follow. Each gardener has some advice to offer, and there are plant and design tips to help you along.

Basics

Before you even begin to plan your garden, clear the decks by addressing the following points.

BYLAWS

Check out local bylaws to see if any prevent plants of a certain height, planting in ditches, and any other regulations that might influence your design. Most municipalities have lists of illegal noxious weeds (which vary from place to place). There are probably height restrictions on fences or hedges, which will be lower in the front than for back gardens, or rules about the height of garden ornaments or corner plantings that might restrict traffic visibility.

Few municipalities mind garden extensions on boulevards or the city-owned frontage as long as they're properly cared for – in fact, residents are usually expected to maintain these bits of property at their own expense, whether they're grass or plants. Minor infractions often slip past the bylaw officer's notice, as long as the garden is a benefit to the neighborhood and there are no complaints from neighbors.

Altering the grade of a property, or a ditch or swale, will be a no-no if it detrimentally affects water runoff. More stringent rules governing exterior paint color, materials for pathways and steps, or even plant choices, may exist in condominium developments, gated communities and some suburbs. In the district of Oak Bay (a suburb of Victoria, British Columbia), for example, residents wanting to plant a front garden on city property adjoining their lot, even if it's inside a municipal sidewalk, must submit a landscape plan for approval and sign an agreement ensuring the proper maintenance of the garden.

NEIGHBORS

Prepare your neighbors. Tell them you plan to take out all or some of your grass and describe the kind of garden you expect to put in. If they seem receptive and you can do it without preaching, talk about the environmental advantages of a biodiverse garden as opposed to a grass monoculture. Mention that an attractively landscaped front garden can increase property values. Assure them your lot will be uprooted for as little time as possible and then live up to your promise: get the job done as quickly as you can, in stages if necessary, and clean up after every stage. This way your front yard won't look more like a construction zone than the beautiful garden it will eventually be.

UNDERGROUND

Check out the location of hydro and telephone wires, both overhead and underground, so you don't interfere with their presence when putting in potentially tall trees or shrubs that require deep planting holes. Deal with problems like bad drainage before you get down to planting. If you want underground irrigation or wiring for night lights, install it before pathways and plants go in.

Hard Surfaces

Before you tackle the garden, look at your house and assess its assets and liabilities. As many of the gardeners on these pages discovered, entranceways, steps and pathways often need attention before the garden itself can be addressed. The biggest complaint is narrow, steep concrete steps, a mingy entrance pad put in by the original builder and a narrow concrete sidewalk that goes straight from A to B, taking the shortest route from the driveway or the street to the front door. Keep in mind that paths, paving and steps are the floors of your outdoor space and as important as the carpet or hardwood indoors. Choose new materials that reflect the style of your house and its setting.

ENTRANCE PAD

Enlarging a concrete entrance stoop isn't usually a big problem. Use the original as a base and add a larger slab to the top, supporting it with walls of concrete blocks or bricks at the extended sides and front. If shrubs are not going to hide the concrete, disguise it with something that fits in with your house style, such as a thin covering of stucco. Top the larger stoop with the surface you've decided upon: mortared flagstone, wood planks, commercial pavers or whatever suits the style of your house and garden.

STEPS

For an entrance with a leisurely, welcoming feeling, make the steps as wide and generous as you can. In turn, the steps should extend the full length of the entrance pad, and the path leading up to them should also be as wide. It's crucial to make steps a uniform height, or you'll invite falls.

There's a magic formula to follow when you're installing steps: twice the height of the riser plus the tread should equal 26 inches. To be both comfortable and safe, risers should be no less than 4 inches and no more than 8 inches high, and treads no less than 9 inches deep. Using the formula, then, steps that are 4 inches high require a tread 18 inches deep – a leisurely ascent indeed. One more step rule: all steps need a teensy downward slope of ⅛ to ¼ of an inch to allow water to drain away.

An entrance to the house that's considerably above grade can look forbidding, especially if the steps are narrow and steep. For a more graceful look and a sense of arrival, consider a "staircase" with a spacious landing between two sets of steps that turn at a right angle to join with the entrance walk. Be as generous as you can with the width and depth of the stairs and landing. An alternative would be to raise the soil at the foundation almost to the level of the entrance pad, tapering it down gradually to the pathway; or retaining it with rocks to create a rock garden. With a wide entrance pad and steps, this will give the illusion that the front door is not as high as it is, especially with a wide entrance pad and steps.

Steps must be flat and safe. Concrete is dependable, if a little dull. Mold your own steps and mix small pebbles into the concrete, allowing them to show on the surface (this is called exposed aggregate). Or imprint the wet

Wide, curving paths are more gracious and welcoming than those laid out on the straight and narrow. Here, the tumbled edges of granite cobblestones suit the billowy cottage plants, barely reining in exuberant cranesbill (*Geranium*), chives (*Allium schoenoprasum*) and periwinkle (*Vinca minor*).

Paths

No rule says you have to follow the original route of the front path. Definitely make it wider, give it a curve or two, make it into a circle or relocate it altogether. For example, you could move the path from entering your garden at the front sidewalk to a side entry off the driveway. Paths that run straight from the gate to the front door usually look severe, but there are exceptions. The path in the secret courtyard garden on page 191 is so well integrated into the overall garden, with a design that echoes the mullions of the windows and the shape of the pond, that one would never consider it uninviting.

concrete with a pattern. Flat stone or brick make ideal steps. Although they may allow dust to be tracked into the house, steps of fine gravel combined with wood edging and risers have a casual appeal. Wood is bold and informal and can be painted or stained to complement the house.

Don't be a slave to stone or plain concrete for pathways. Choose material that will complement your garden style.

The angled raised boardwalk set above a dry stream of pebbles, rocks and tufts of ornamental grasses resembles a nature trail.

- Wood is casual and has a country feeling. It does require more maintenance than harder materials and can be slippery when wet, but in a ferny, shady front garden a raised wood-slat pathway can make you feel you're wandering though a nature trail.
- Poured concrete embedded with flat pebbles, which can be arranged in a mosaic-like pattern or spread at random, provides a casual effect.
- Wet concrete imprinted with leaf and shell patterns or geometric designs is a creative choice.
- Concrete with exposed aggregates looks sophisticated and modern.
- Crushed tile and pea gravel make lovely cottagey paths and are less expensive than flagstone.

- For a more formal look and sturdier surface on an entrance path, embed the gravel with square concrete stepping stones or random flagstones.
- Clay brick is timeless, laid in any of the classic patterns: basketweave, running bond, diagonal. To prevent cracking or flaking if you live where soil freezes in winter, set bricks in a deep layer of gravel (12 inches if you can manage it) topped with builder's sand. A 3- to 4-inch base is necessary in other climates.

Style

Creating a front garden may not seem much different to making one in the back, but there are a few significant distinctions. To begin with, a front garden is essentially a public place, one that will be seen by your neighbors and anyone who passes by. Make it one you're proud to share. A front garden can also be viewed from several sides – from the street and your next door neighbors' yards as well as from your house. You need to take all these different sight lines into consideration.

The gardener's tried-and-true formula for planting borders backed by a hedge or a fence, with the tall stuff at the back graduating down to edging plants at the front, doesn't often work in a garden that can be viewed from all sides. You may be able to create a background on one side of your front garden with a hedge or bank of shrubs, but much depends on the site and your neighbors, who may feel isolated by a barrier of large plants.

When developing your garden's style, aim for a look that not only suits your house and personal taste but fits with the character of the neighborhood. Every neighborhood has its own intrinsic personality and you don't want to introduce jarring change, especially if your new garden is going to stray from a conservative lawn-and-foundation-plant mindset. In other words, a cottage garden will fit fine in a modest neighborhood of relatively small houses, but an ostentatious circular driveway with lions at the gate and a huge fish spouting water into a central pond will be sure to draw stares and annoyed harrumphs.

Borrow ideas wherever you find them, including this book. Clip photos from magazines. While on walks, garden tours, or vacation, take snapshots of favorite gardens, beds or features like arbors and pergolas. Where do you suppose other gardeners get their ideas? Keep a file and your own style will gradually emerge.

Creating a detailed design on paper can be counterproductive to gardeners like me who need to get out on the site to visualize the end result, but it's initially beneficial to at least make a lot plan to scale and mark existing features. Note trees and the spread of their canopy structures like the house, garage and existing fences; and the shape and size of the pathways and steps you intend to keep. Also indicate outdoor power outlets, overhead and underground wires, boggy, sunny or dry areas, and the garden's orientation: north, south east or west. Getting this basic site information down on paper helps you figure out the nature of your space and can alert you to potential problems, like heavy shade in one corner or a bog in another. It will make you think about what you need to do first and may even inspire an overall design.

Once you decide on a garden style, stick to it. It will help you choose plants, accessories and structures that harmonize with the whole. If you're thinking modern, for example, you'll be less likely to purchase an ornate piece of formal sculpture you simply adore but that won't fit into a modern setting in a million years.

A tip, of the last-but-not-least variety: some of the best front yard gardens just evolve. I know a couple that kept growing out from the foundation planting, getting wider and wider each year until they reached the street. The neighbors didn't even know what was happening. And another was originally made up of island beds that got bigger and bigger, leaving narrower and narrower strips of grass between them. These strips eventually became grass pathways and the beds took over. This isn't a bad approach to planning a garden if you're stuck for ideas: on a plan of your lot, draw several circles or shapes in the grassy area and keep widening them until the spaces between are reduced to paths.

Paths made with clay brick create a timeless look. The arching branches of a golden chain tree (*Laburnum anagyroides*) in glorious full bloom punctuate the entrance and entice visitors to step in to the garden. Lupines (*Lupinus*) and white bleeding heart (*Dicentra spectabilis* 'Alba') add more sparkle.

"IF WE EVER MOVE from here, I'm taking this garden with me," says Suzanne Scott of her front yard rock garden. "It's going to be written into the sales agreement."

She's only half joking. Many people do uproot and transport plants to their new gardens when they move, but that's hardly possible with the huge limestone rocks in the Scotts' front yard. Suzanne says this to illustrate her attachment to the garden, completed in a mere four weeks in 1998. "I didn't know it, but Michael was having a surprise birthday party for me and had secretly told our landscaper the contract was his only if he had it finished on time," laughs Suzanne. "I couldn't figure out why he was so anxious to get it done."

She and Michael and their young family had moved into the gracious old house in 1995, and within a couple of years decided one of their priorities was a front-garden facelift. First, to allow more air circulation ("and so we could see what was happening on the street"), Michael and a friend replaced the solid wood porch front with straight spindles, took out the concrete steps and built wider wooden ones.

In the meantime, Suzanne was dreaming up garden designs for the grassy property, which sloped slightly from the street down to the front walk. "You have to do this: dream about it, mull it over, before you know what you really want esthetically," she says. "It's a process that takes time, and you have to let it." She decided she wanted a wide sweeping path and substantial limestone rocks to hold back the soil of the slope – a rock garden, in effect. "I

Suzanne Scott knew her front garden needed a facelift, but mulled over several ideas before tackling the project. She decided on a wide sweeping path, limestone rocks to hold back the slight slope, and drifts of ground covers, such as Japanese spurge (*Pachysandra terminalis*) and moss phlox (*Phlox subulata*), which are planted in an arc. "I wanted it to be natural and easy to maintain, but at the same time something I could change as the years went by," she says.

Birth of a Front Yard Garden

Dundas, Ontario

wanted it to be natural and easy to maintain, but at the same time something I could change as the years went by, with lots of green but a few different color schemes."

The rock garden was definitely not a task for Michael and his friend. Professional help was in order and the Scotts eventually decided on a landscape architect recommended by a relative, but only after viewing the architect's own garden and seeing his portfolio.

Once hired, he discovered a drainage problem the Scotts were barely aware of: the annoying flow of water into their next-door neighbor's driveway during heavy rains was caused by the general slope of the Scotts' property from the west side to the east, (or from right to left in the picture), not from the slope toward the house from the street. This problem had to be addressed first, or risk diverting even more water the neighbor's way.

The solution was simple enough: the downspout on the eavestrough of the Scotts' house was moved from the east, or driveway side, to the west, and connected to an underground reservoir near the side of the house. It collects the extra rainwater, which also drains into it through weeping tiles installed under the rock garden, and holds it till it gradually seeps into the soil. "Hiring a professional can seem like a big issue sometimes," says Suzanne, "but he helped us identify a problem we only had an inkling existed."

Above: Halfway through the process, with the rocks and topsoil in place and the ground prepared for the flagstone pathway and border beds. Below: Almost the same view, with the flagstones laid and the garden flourishing with moss phlox, bergenia and variegated hostas. Opposite: A lush bed of Japanese spurge (*Pachysandra terminalis*) makes a green skirt under a mature evergreen in the Scotts' front garden. Suzanne is training English ivy and climbing hydrangea up its massive trunk.

Another professional, a landscape contractor, was required to install the eavestrough and reservoir, the weeping tiles under the rocks, and to construct the rockery. Three quotes were obtained. "One was so high we figured he didn't want the job," says Suzanne. The other two were close, but one of them was a hands-down winner. "There was a good feeling between us the minute we met, and we spent some time chatting so he'd get to know our tastes and personalities. He was a one-man show with a summer crew, and very creative. As we went along we had to make adjustments for budget reasons, and he was always on our wavelength with his solutions."

The day the rocks were delivered she knew he'd definitely been the right choice. He'd handpicked them and they were perfect: big, old and characterful, sprouting lichen and tiny ferns in the crevices. "But all the neighbors came out of their houses and just stared at this big pile on the road," says Suzanne. "We were relatively new to the street and I guess they wondered what the heck we were doing. The next-door neighbor was really worried – she'd lived here fifty years and didn't like change. We had a lot of stroking to do – offerings of cookies and cake, and an occasional barbecued steak on a Sunday."

The topsoil was delivered and within a day there was a downpour, washing streams of mud into the neighbor's driveway. They had to start stroking all over again. "But once the garden was in she liked it fine, because she could sit on her front porch and enjoy it, too."

Suzanne kept a close eye on the installation of the rocks, which the contractor put in place himself with his BobCat. "He told me he had karma with rocks, and he was right," she says. He followed the architect's plan, but adjusted it to suit the particular rocks and to widen the curve at the west end of the garden to allow for a sitting area.

"One thing to remember when you have to hire someone to do construction: there are always going to be extras, just like in a house renovation," says Suzanne. "Some of the equipment and the rocks destroyed the grass on the upper level near the road, and that had to be replaced. We

also had underground wiring put in for lights, which we hadn't planned on, and we carried the flagstone around to the side door. It all cost more, which meant we definitely couldn't afford the arbor designed for the entrance into the back." That will be a future project.

The garden looked like it had always been there almost from the moment it was finished, and in the four summers since it's really taken off, at least in part because of the rich topsoil brought in to build up the garden and fill between the rocks. The neighbors are envious of the success of the Japanese spurge, and the pretty variegated hostas have totally filled in their allotted space. The rhododendrons, moss phlox, flowering cherry and pink flowering dogwood are glorious in spring. Summer brings a subtle blend of shade-loving plants such as dwarf goatsbeard, astilbe, ferns and ivy, as well as bergenia, lady's mantle, echinacea, sedum and Japanese anemone. Plants flow over the rocks and grow along the edges of the pathway. "Because it's lower than the street, this is really a garden meant for us," Suzanne says. "On summer evenings we take our chairs down to the little sitting area, and we can barely be seen."

It's important to have some idea of what you want before you start on a major garden project that's going to require structural work, she says, and then to research the people you hire, and choose those whose ideas fit with yours and who you feel you can work with. "I don't think we've ever had anything go so smoothly as this garden," she says. It left everyone in such good humor, in fact, that the contractor and the crew were invited to her surprise party, and arrived carrying gifts of plants for the garden. ■

Late spring-blooming rhododendrons thrive in the rich soil in the Scotts' garden; acid-green blooms on lady's mantle (*Alchemilla mollis*) brighten the semi-shady corner. A blue glazed earthenware pot holds tuberous begonias, which will provide summer color after the rhododendrons fade.

Plants

Spring
crocus (*Crocus*)
flowering almond (*Prunus triloba*)
moss phlox (*Phlox subulata*)
pink flowering dogwood (*Cornus florida* f. *rubra*)
rhododendrons
tulips

Early to Mid-Summer
astilbe (*Astilbe*)
dwarf goatsbeard (*Aruncus aesthusifolius*)
lady's mantle (*Alchemilla mollis*)
purple coneflower (*Echinacea purpurea*)

Fall
'The Giant' colchicum (*Colchicum* 'The Giant')
'Queen Charlotte' Japanese anemone (*Anemone hybrida* 'Queen Charlotte')

All-Season Ground Covers
Baltic ivy (*Hedera helix* 'Baltica')
bergenia (*Bergenia cordifolia*)
hosta (*Hosta* 'So Sweet')
Japanese spurge (*Pachysandra terminalis*)
sedum (*Sedum spectabile*)
sword fern (*Polystichum*)
wood fern (*Dryopteris*)

Japanese spurge (*Pachysandra terminalis*)

Chapter Five

Cottage Gardens

Once upon a time the cottage garden was not a fashion statement, but a necessity. In little plots in front of cottages in the eighteenth-century English countryside,

laborers and farmers grew plants for sustenance and survival – vegetables and fruits for the table, herbs for medicinal and culinary use, flowers to attract bees and other pollinators – and kept a chicken or two and a goat. Hollyhocks, wild roses and cosmos might have been grown to provide nosegays for the gardener's pleasure, but they took their place between the cabbages and carrots.

With the help of turn-of-the-century British garden designers like Gertrude Jekyll and William Robinson, gardeners romanticized the traditional cottage garden and transformed it into high style. Today's cottage gardens may look as random as their predecessors, but most depend on artfully planned combinations of flowers: old-fashioned choices such as roses, lavender, daphne, primroses, sunflowers, spring bulbs, phlox, sweet peas and pinks. They fill the spaces, growing in clumps of harmonious colors, falling over fences and tumbling over gravel pathways.

As important as the flowers is the cottage itself. Such a loose garden seldom looks its best against a formal, pillared mansion or an ultra-modern ranch bungalow. But they fit beautifully with pretty houses of pleasing pastel colors and houses with shutters or picket fences, dormers and gingerbread. Exceptions can work, of course, as long as care is taken to match the accessories of the garden – the paths, arbors, bird baths or fountains – to the style and materials of the house. The garden and the cottage should look like they were made for each other.

Picket fences, gravel pathways and stucco houses are hallmarks of cottage gardens. So are old-fashioned plants like the mauvey-blue iris (*Iris sibirica*), single wild roses and yellow daylilies in the garden opposite, which are complemented by a mauve rhododendron and a lilac. Several varieties of Austin roses grow in the cottage garden above, as well as yellow daylilies (*Hemerocallis*) and white daisies (*Leucanthemum*).

LIZA DROZDOV'S front garden pleases her, and apparently others like it, too. "People often slow down as they drive by to see what's blooming," Liza says. In spring it's chionodoxa, scilla, snowdrops, tulips and crocus; over the summer lilies, roses, allium, wisteria, clematis, peonies and shasta daisies grow in profusion; in fall Japanese anemones, asters and aconite complement the season's orange and gold leaves. Liza's house looks like a fairy-tale cottage: a quaint pale-blue stucco house surrounded by drifts of blue, lavender, pink and white flowers accented with purple smoke tree, heuchera and penstemon.

But the scene wasn't always so charming. When Liza and her husband, Adrian Bell, bought the tiny rundown house in 1991, it was the ugliest on the block ("perhaps in the town," says Liza), covered with dark red fake-brick siding set off with slatted plastic awnings. There was no garden to speak of, only a lawn of patchy grass that grew right up to the foundations of the house.

"I had dreams of an abundant cottage garden, but I was a novice and started with no real plan," says Liza. "Much of my success is blind luck." The modest Liza also admits to an impatient streak, which made her start her garden before she and Adrian had the money to improve the exterior of the house. "It was such an eyesore, we wanted to make it look as though someone who cared lived there. So right away I dug beds in the front and the side of the house, which face south and south-west, the best place for a garden, and I double-dug them in the old-fashioned way, two spades deep," she says. (Liza is energetic and strong, as well as impatient.) She added manure, compost and leaf mold

Late spring in Liza Drozdov's garden features giant purple allium (*Allium* 'Globemaster'), yellow daylilies (*Hemerocallis*), pale pink double and darker pink peony cultivars (*Paeonia*) and feathery pink meadow rue (*Thalictrum aquilegifolium*). An 'Alchymist' rose, a tall apricot-orange shrub rose climbs beside the front door, while a Japanese wisteria (*Wisteria floribunda*) frames the window.

A Renovated Cottage

Oakville, Ontario

to improve the sandy soil and, willy nilly, planted her favorite peonies, foxgloves, roses, balloon flowers, daylilies and scabiosa.

The original beds were narrower than the present wide plantings, which is the way most gardeners start, stealing more and more space as their gardening ambitions grow. Within three years, as the plants were becoming established and beginning to take off, Liza and Adrian decided to stucco the house.

"I asked the contractor how this might affect the garden," says Liza, "and he shrugged and said some stucco might fall on it. So I decided to take precautions. I took down the climbing roses and the wisteria – thank goodness they were still young enough to be flexible! – and wrapped them and the shrubs in burlap. I trimmed back the perennials and covered them with five-gallon pots. Some I tied with twine, silly me, thinking this might protect them."

When Liza came home from work the day after the construction crew began work, the garden looked like a war zone, with equipment everywhere, some of it strewn over the plants that had been so carefully protected. So Liza removed the plants from the fray – she dug them up and jammed them into plastic bags, then laid them out in a far corner of the backyard, where they stayed till the stucco was finished. "I barely had time to replant before freeze-up,"

A dozen years ago, Liza Drozdov's house was the ugliest one on the block, with fake-brick siding and plastic awnings. Liza and her husband converted it to a sweet cottage with a stop-and-stare garden. It includes clumps of single pink peonies (*Paeonia*) on either side of the front walk that bloom like a mass of giant butterflies, as well as the plants mentioned on the previous page.

says Liza. "Thank goodness it was a mild winter – I lost only one plant."

Around the house Liza had put in mostly blue flowers because it's her favorite color, but once the stucco was on – in a shade of blue Liza still thinks is too "timid" – the flowers faded into the background. So she introduced brighter pinks and mauves, spiked with white and deeper maroons. The colors of the house trim were also decided upon after the stucco was applied. "We really got lucky with the door,"

Liza says. "Who'd have thought periwinkle blue would work with the grayed blues on the rest of the house? We kept considering red, or maybe black, then one day Adrian said enough, no more waffling, and went to the store and came home with a can of paint. That's how a lot of things happen around here."

Liza gardens from the hip, you might say, as do many of us. She moved her rhododendrons three times before they ended up at the east side of the house, nestled under a hedge of bittersweet. Early in her gardening years she thought globe cedars on each side of the front steps and a couple of upright cedars at the corners of the house would add winter interest and make a statement. Once they were in she realized how mundane they were, like every other foundation planting she'd ever seen. Soon they disappeared in favor of deciduous shrubs and grasses, which have winter form though no greenery. Another year she put in a lovely wide gravel path curving from the driveway alongside the garden to a gate leading to the backyard, and then had to dig up part of it to run electrical service to the garage.

The new wiring was necessary because she and Adrian had decided to move the garage, which was too close to street. So they set it on rollers and gradually moved it back. "Just the way the pyramids were built, only in this case we were the slaves!" laughs Liza. "Our neighbors took a pool on how long it would take to fall over, but we moved it without incident." Moving the garage left the entire west side of the house open, creating a bigger garden in full sun.

Meanwhile, the garden around the front door was evolving: each year Liza would steal a few more inches of space until there was only about 10 square feet of grass on each side of the sidewalk. The lilies, thalictrum and aconite she'd put in to hide the foundation had grown so tall they were hiding the windowbox plantings. So out came the grass. "I'd planted the front the traditional way, with tall stuff at the back and some shorter things near the front. But I couldn't see this garden from inside," says Liza. "Only passersby got to look at it." So she reversed the process and moved tall plants – some transplanted roses, allium, Christmas rose and lilies – to the sidewalk, adding shorter varieties nearer the house.

"It's so jam-packed you can't even step into it now," says Liza. "But that's fine. I never really liked the grass anyway. It's a colossal waste of time – people panic about white grubs and spray for this and that, and for what? I'd rather have flowers." ■

Liza kept stealing inches of grass from the front yard garden until she finally took it all out. She reconfigured the garden, moving tall plants from under the window to the street side, where they could be seen from the house. In this picture, taken one year after the one opposite, alliums and yellow daylilies grow in front of tall blue bellflower (*Campanula*).

MANY GARDENERS take as long to plan a front yard garden as they do to dig up the grass and put in the plants. It can take years. But Ferne Taylor is a quick study: her garden went in the summer she took possession of her house, despite a serious challenge – an asphalt parking pad covering the entire front yard.

Ferne had rented the upstairs apartment in the clapboard house for eighteen years before the owner decided to sell. She loved the place and quickly snapped it up. "It's a beautiful house, but I was so embarrassed by the front I sometimes couldn't bear to tell people where I lived," says Ferne. "I wanted the asphalt out as soon as possible."

Ferne took possession in the spring of 1988, feeling some urgency to make changes right away: her twin sister, Heather – a serious gardener, unlike Ferne – was coming home from the west coast in July for a visit. "I had to do house renovations and fix up the property before she got here," Ferne says.

As the renovations got underway, Ferne tackled the all-grass backyard. First, she moved the car park to behind the house, where a lane offered access to the rear of the property. Then she made a garden in the back, taking out all the grass. "I thoroughly loved it," she says. "I decided I didn't want to spend Saturday mornings cutting grass, and I liked the bees and butterflies, so the front was going to be garden, too."

Meanwhile, the asphalt and the packed gravel substructure was coming out with the help of a crew with jackhammers. Ferne had three truckloads of topsoil brought in to fill the resulting depression, and then enriched it with peat moss and mushroom manure. Next, she installed a wide, deep planter across the front of the house to cover the foundation and make a transition between house and garden, and built a simple picket fence.

"I planned it carefully, doing up plans at night, because I didn't want it to look pretentious," Ferne says. "I wanted to carry out a cottage look." Her neighbors watched with wonder, and commented on how the changes she was making enhanced the neighborhood. Except for the man next

A City Cottage

Charlottetown,
Prince Edward Island

Opposite: Once an ugly asphalt parking pad, Ferne Taylor's cottage garden is now the pride of the neighborhood. Its white picket fence – designed by Ferne – and carefully chosen plants are part of the new streetscape. The yellow daylilies (*Hemerocallis*) growing in front of the fence pick up the color of the house. Below: The view from the house. The position of small trees, such as the globe-shaped Norway maple (*Acer platanoides* 'Globosum') near the street, was carefully mapped out on paper before the garden was put in. Pale gold wallflower (*Erysimum cheiri*) echoes the bright green ferns and yellow daylilies.

The garden's northeast exposure means it receives more shade than sun, so ferns and hostas, like those marching along the raised bed in front of the house, above, are favored plants. The yellow daylilies, Siberian iris and moss phlox also do well. Canadian-bred 'Explorer' roses and lilacs below and opposite, were chosen because they're hardy and long-blooming.

door. He said her fence shouldn't be allowed on a street with just lawns, and he was going to ask city hall to order her to remove it. "Nothing was done, but he still complains about the 'mess' I have over here," Ferne chuckles.

She kept the original concrete front walk, which had cracked over the years, and planted tough ground covers in the spaces. The plants tie the walk to the garden, and the chamomile and thyme smell good when walked upon.

The choice of plants was governed by the northeast exposure of the front of the house, which gets direct sun for only about four hours each morning in high summer. Ferns and heathers were the first choices, then daylilies and hostas, using variegated cultivars because they provide a sun-dappled look even when it's shady. The placement of shrubs and large perennials (rhododendrons, astilbe, hydrangeas), and the small trees (a globe-shaped Norway maple and an ash), was drafted out on paper, as was the design of the cedar-chip pathway, which Ferne planned to look like a dry stream bed.

But other plants went in where they seemed to look best, and where they would enhance the loose look of the cottage garden. Many were donated by friends. Some suffered damage when a new roof was installed the following year, which gave Ferne a chance to edit out what didn't look good. "It was just like moving around the living room furniture and discarding what you don't want," laughs Ferne.

After the new terra-cotta colored roof went on in 1999, Ferne decided to streamline her color combinations, starting with the white clapboard on the house. "I decided on yellow because it's happy, even on rainy days." Many of the purple, mauve and pink flowers in the garden are being phased out because they don't bloom long enough or well enough in the shade, and the emphasis is now on light-colored foliage and shade-loving plants, such as the yellow daylilies that complement the house so well and flower nearly all summer.

Ferne feels that doing her garden so quickly was right for her. "If I hadn't, I might have got used to it looking the way it did, and ended up with nothing," she says. "I decided to go for it and owe the bank, but I get to enjoy it – now." ▪

The small bed centering the path to Anne Kotyk's woodland cottage grew from a serendipitous pile of sand placed there during early renovations. The shape appealed to Anne and she planted it with a burning bush (*Euonymus alatus*) that's still providing stunning crimson fall color. In spring (as shown here) the generally shady garden glows with varied greens, deep blue grape hyacinths (*Muscari*) and white foamflower (*Tiarella cordifolia*), as seen at right, plus dainty white daffodils (*Narcissus*) with swept-back petals and sky-blue forget-me-nots (*Myosotis*).

A Cottage in the Woods

Algonquin Island, Toronto

THE GENESIS of this garden on Algonquin Island, one of a series of small islands off the south shore of Toronto, was a pile of sand. That's a simplification, of course, because the gardener, Anne Kotyk, had a larger vision: to create a lush front yard environment with form, height and textures instead of the poor growth of grass and the few trees inherited when she and her husband bought the tiny cottage nearly twenty years ago. She wanted a garden she could walk through, enjoying the plants and the ambience in all seasons of the year.

The vision hadn't quite taken shape in her mind when her husband, while doing some foundation repair, piled the excavated sand at the front of the house. "The pile took a nice sort of arc shape," Anne says, "and I thought it would make a perfect bed." The original bed still contains the burning bush Anne planted there when she made the garden, and it continues to light the generally shady space with stunning red color in the fall.

About the same time, another bed went in at the front of the house, where the low deck outside the French doors to the main part of the house now stands (the house has undergone extensive renovations). Then she created the bed to the left of the branched flagstone path. "I kept adding beds without any real plan, and the garden just grew," Anne says. Now it covers the whole 40-foot depth of the front yard. In spring it is a lovely sight, with narcissus, grape hyacinths, forget-me-nots, primulas, violets and foamflowers.

A large eastern cottonwood, a fast-growing tree native to the islands, and a crab apple provide dappled shade, with some heavier shade coming from the 40-foot (and still growing) spruce trees across the street to the west. "From the beginning, I've treated it mainly as a foliage garden," Anne says. She planted azaleas, Japanese maples and Pagoda dogwood, 'Nanum' viburnum for spring fragrance, leucothoe for its drooping, pearl-like flowers, summersweet and *Kirengeshoma palmata*, which has maple-like leaves and beautiful little yellow bell flowers late in the season. Evergreens abound in many forms from dwarf to tall,

although the 'Skyrocket' junipers Anne planted at the corners of the house in the early days ("because that is what everyone else did," she laughs) have gone.

The little pond hidden under the Japanese maple near the front path is an invisible feature. "It's just a plastic container with a pump, with stones set on a grid above the water," says Anne, "but it's so hidden the postman keeps looking around for the babbling brook when he delivers the mail." ∎

A Colorful Cottage

Here the cottage itself is just as important as the flowers in sending an inviting message. On Algonquin Island, off the southern shore of Toronto, it's the home of a color consultant who's matched the exuberant colors of the cottage with the plants in her garden.

A Roadside Cottage

Despite the lack of ground space, the Dundas, Ontario, garden, above, is a traffic stopper. The gardener has capitalized on her simple dormered cottage with color. The rambling orange trumpet creeper vine (*Campsis radicans*) clings to the yellow-painted brick and climbs over the eaves. She's kept the planting simple, and used the "dot" approach to place the purple coneflower (*Echinacea purpurea*) and single rose.

A Modern Cottage

Perfectly placed pink Asiatic lilies, roses and a lacy Japanese maple (*Acer palmatum*) in a relatively new garden in Oakville, Ontario, below, tie in beautifully with the more formal quality of the surrounding neighborhood. The path of pea gravel, the wood shaving mulch and flat entranceway stones fit nicely with the cottage style and match the casual mood of the house.

Creating a Cottage Garden

A good cottage garden is an irresistible package of color, scent and atmosphere. There are a few rules to observe when creating one, but at its heart a cottage garden should look like it just grew. It's informal, sensual and small, sometimes even tiny, but above all, like the warm and welcoming Oakville, Ontario, garden opposite, it reflects the personality of its owners.

House

- An ancient thatched roof would be the ideal (and historically correct) foil for a cottage garden, but gingerbread, as in the house shown at left, runs a close second.
- Stucco and clapboard fit the cottage style. Brick – especially painted brick – also maintains the casual look.
- The colors used on the house and the trim are important to the overall look. They should blend with the garden's colors, or boldly beckon the eye.

Materials

- Informal paths and driveways look best. Use crushed tile, gravel or limestone screenings, random flagstone, cobblestone or old brick. Packed earth or wood chips also fit the style.
- Fences and gates are part of the cottage tradition (originally used to keep in the goats and chickens). Use split rails, weathered or painted pickets and woven willow. Simple metal fences also work.
- River pebbles, rocks, sea shells and shingles make good edgings.

Accessories

- Choose wicker, willow, wood or worn metal furniture. Most important: be sure it's comfortable.
- Statuary, of the classical or folksy garden-gnome variety, is seldom seen in cottage gardens.
- Use clay pots, bushel baskets, old tin cans and the like as planters. Give them a thin wash of white or black paint for an aged or recycled look.
- Make plant supports of twigs tied like teepees and arbors of sturdy peeled poles.

Cottage gardens are admired for their lush tumble of flowers and warm, welcoming mood, in which the house as well as the garden play a role. The house and garden above, on a busy residential street just off the busier main street of Oakville, Ontario, was built less than a decade ago but looks like it belongs to the last century. A wide verandah where one can watch the world go by is furnished with white wicker armchairs cushioned in blue. Porch planter boxes are crammed with purple petunias. The wide rock garden, adjoining a patch of lawn, is filled with boxweed (*Buxus*) and complementary creeping pink baby's breath (*Gypsophila repens*), cerise impatiens and blue bellflower (*Campanula*). Opposite: An old-fashioned house and garden in downtown Toronto draw the eye away from a stark brick wall next door. Lilies and daylilies, ivies and ferns fill the garden space, with annuals like impatiens growing among them.

Plants

Spring

alpine forget-me-not (*Myosotis alpestris*)

basket-of-gold (*Aurinia saxatilis*)

bistort (*Persicaria bistorta* 'Superba')

bleeding heart (*Dicentra*)

Canterbury bells (*Campanula medium*)

clumps of crocus (*Crocus ancyrensis, C. sieberii* 'Firefly', *C. vernus* 'Joan of Arc')

columbine (*Aquilegia*)

English daisy (*Bellis perennis*)

moss phlox (*Phlox subulata*)

naturalized daffodils (*Narcissus* 'Avalanche', 'Jetfire', 'Pipit', *N. poeticus* var. *recurvus*)

pansies (*Viola x wittrockiana*)

pennyroyal (*Mentha pulegium*)

primrose (*Primula*)

pussy toes (*Antennaria dioica*)

rock cress (*Aubrieta*)

snowdrops (*Galanthus nivalis*)

species tulips (*Tulipa tarda, T. sylvestris, T. biflora, T. pulchella, T. humilis*)

violets (*Viola*)

Purple iris and golden creeping Jenny

White foxglove, purple hybrid salvia, California poppies, coral bells

Early to Mid-Summer

annual poppies: opium poppy (*Papaver somniferum*), Flanders poppy (*P. rhoeas*), *P. commutatum*

baby's breath (*Gypsophila paniculata*)

bloody cranesbill (*Geranium sanguineum*)

dwarf goatsbeard (*Aruncus aesthusifolius*)

lemon daylily (*Hemerocallis lilioasphodelus*)

love-lies-bleeding (*Amaranthus caudatus*)

old roses (*Rosa alba, R. bourbon, R. centifolia, R. damask*)

oxeye daisy (*Leucanthemum vulgare*)

peach-leaved bellflower (*Campanula persicifolia*)

'The Fairy' rose, with yellow and pink Asiatic lilies

sweet or dame's rocket (*Hesperis matronalis*)

'Whirling Butterflies' gaura (*Gaura lindheimeri* 'Whirling Butterflies')

yarrow (*Achillea*)

Late Summer to Fall

angelica (*Angelica gigas*)

anise-hyssop (*Agastache foeniculum*)

black snakeroot (*Cimicifuga racemosa*)

boltonia (*Boltonia asteroides*)

castor bean (*Ricinus communis*)

china aster (*Callistephus chinensis*)

cupid's dart (*Catananche caerulea*)

four o'clock (*Mirabilis jalapa*)

hollyhock (*Alcea rosea*)

lavatera (*Lavatera trimestris*)

Mexican sunflower (*Tithonia rotundifolia*)

monkshood (*Aconitum*)

morning glory (*Ipomoea*)

pearly everlasting (*Anaphalis margaritacea*)

rose mallow (*Hibiscus mosheutos*)

stock, gillyflower (*Matthiola incana*)

sunflower (*Helianthus annuus*)

valerian (*Centranthus ruber*)

All-season Annuals

calendula (*Calendula officinalis*)

California poppy (*Eschscholzia californica*)

catchfly (*Silene*)

clarkia or godetia (*Clarkia*)

corn cockle (*Agrostemma githago*)

cornflower, bachelor's buttons (*Centaurea cyanus*)

cosmos (*Cosmos*)

flowering tobacco (*Nicotiana sylvestris*)

heliotrope (*Heliotropium arborescens*)

larkspur (*Consolida ajacis*)

love-in-a-mist (*Nigella damascena*)

painted tongue (*Salpiglossis sinuata*)

sweet pea (*Lathyrus odoratus*)

zinnia (*Zinnia*)

Herbs

Herbs are important members of cottage gardens. Choose decorative varieties like those listed below. Don't forget to include other ornamental edibles as edgings, such as colored or textured greens: 'Red Sails' or 'Oak Leaf' lettuces, purslane (*Portulaca oleracea*), and ornamental kale (*Brassica oleracea* var. *acephala*).

bronze fennel (*Foeniculum vulgare* 'Atropurpureum')

bush basil (*Ocimum basilicum minimum*)

curled parsley (*Petroselinum crispum*)

dill (*Anethum graveolens*)

garlic (*Allium sativum*)

purple basil (*Ocimum basilicum* 'Purple Ruffles')

rosemary (*Rosmarinus officinalis*)

tricolor sage (*Salvia officinalis* 'Tricolor')

Above: Pink cosmos, sunflowers, French marigolds. Below: Deep maroon hollyhocks (*Alcea rosea*), white and pink cleomes (*Cleome hassleriana*), purple annual Clary sage (*Salvia viridis*) and marigolds grow among tomatoes and kale.

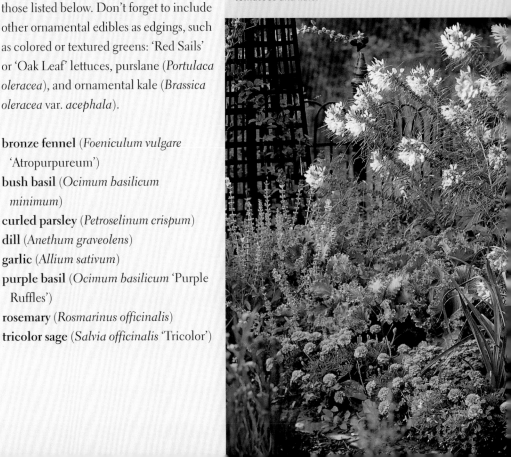

Chapter Six

Small City Gardens

There's something special about really small gardens. They're what many of us have if we live in urban environments cheek-by-jowl with our neighbors. They can

have more personality than a large garden simply because their style is condensed into the essence of the owner's personality.

That's assuming the owner has allowed the garden to reflect his or her personality, of course. I love the inner-city front yard vegetable gardens I've seen because they're so practical, but I also admire beautifully designed formal gardens because they say the owners really care about how their garden looks in the neighborhood. I laugh at funky narrow sidewalk gardens with potted plants surrounded by plastic flamingoes or gnomes because I know the gardener is making a statement. I appreciate a flowery cottage garden because I relate to the owner – she's like me, I know.

Many people consider small gardens hard to work with because there's so little space, but nothing could be further from the truth. Small gardens are the easiest of all to design. The secret lies in knowing what purpose you want the garden to fulfill. Should it, in fact, be your source of vegetables? Then make it so, as a row-upon-row planting of comestibles or a formal potager. Is it another room to your house, perhaps the entrance, or a place to sit? Then give it a bench backed by a group of shrubs. Is it just for fun? Let yourself go – do the flamingo or gnome thing, and change the arrangement when you feel like it.

Your small front garden should be one of life's little pleasures. Take some inspiration from the gardeners in this chapter – none of whom would be caught dead with a garden of concrete and grass.

Even if they're space challenged, tiny gardens offer unlimited opportunity for expressing yourself with color. Opposite: The riotous colors of golden chain tree (*Laburnum anagyroides*), rose and purple lupines (*Lupinus*) and white bleeding heart (*Dicentra spectabilis* 'Alba'). Above: Red and yellow tulips and daffodils, white trilliums (*Trillium grandiflorum*) and tiny blue forget-me-nots (*Myosotis*).

GARDENING MAY BE Judith Adam's grand obsession, but she maintains a sense of humor. She can hardly restrain her throaty laugh as she tells the story of the maple tree that once shaded her front yard.

It was a lovely tree, as maple trees tend to be even as they cast shade over a garden's sun-loving plants, but although it appeared to be on her neighbor's property it was officially city-owned, so neither the Adams nor their next-door neighbors could do much about its leafy presence. Nevertheless, Judith complained to the neighbor constantly. "At least five phone calls a day," she exaggerates. "'Can you cut it down? At least trim it back? Do *something* with it?' They'd say, 'Well Judith, you can complain to us all you want, but it's a city tree. It's not up to us.'"

So, being a practical person, Judith decided to change that side to a shade garden. That was about four years ago, and the garden was due for some renovation anyway, having been in place for more than ten years as the maple tree grew larger and larger. Judith is also decisive, so once she'd made a plan she moved quickly.

"And about two weeks after the new plants were in, I was driving down the street one day coming home from work, and there it was ... gone! Gone! The tree was gone! And there I was, with a shade garden in the sun. My poor neighbors had got sick of my complaints and finally went to the city and convinced someone the tree was sick and had to come down."

All in all, it worked out all right, Judith says. She had to move a few plants into shadier conditions, and a few hostas turned yellow and dried up, but most plants adjusted better than they'd expected.

But the story continues ...

In Judith Adam's garden, a raised round bed was encircled with a pathway of granite setts. Mauve chives (*Allium schoenoprasum*) and bergenia have grown in around the stones. To the right of the path grows purple-blue columbine (*Aquilegia*), an unnamed white rose and variegated golden sage (*Salvia officinalis* 'Icterina') used as an edging.

Let There Be Light
Toronto, Ontario

"Shortly thereafter," Judith says, pausing like a performer, "the city decided to move the lamppost, which had been two houses farther down. It went to the place the maple tree had been. I wasn't pleased about that, either. But once I'd quit complaining I had to admit they'd provided me with light to garden at night. Now I can garden at midnight with no problem. I can easily see every plant on the property. I can plant, prune – whatever – any time I want."

Judith is still laughing about her rotten luck. However, the story comes with a silver lining. "Actually," she says, "I like to prune at night, because you see the whole tree, its shape. You don't get hung up on the little branches here and there. You get a sense of the outline, the form." It's rather like seeing the forest instead of just the trees.

Judith and her husband, Peter, moved into the historical 1889 house in 1978. Their first priority was the exterior: removing the white paint that covered the beautiful rose and cream brick, having a new door built to reproduce the original one and replacing the narrow poured-concrete steps with a more gracious, wide entrance of creamy limestone. "We had to remove the foundation plantings so they could acid-wash the brick, and things gradually progressed from there," Judith says. "By the mid-1980s we were ready to tackle the garden. There was a dreadful Chinese elm hedge. It was the first to go. And there was a straight asphalt

Above: The foundation planting includes pale mauve rhododendron, white milky bellflower (*Campanula lactiflora*), a double pink columbine (*Aquilegia*) and a variegated euonymus (*Euonymus fortunei* 'Emerald Gaiety') climbing the house. White peach-leaved bellflower (*Campanula persicifolia*) is in the foreground, and a handsome red Japanese maple (*Acer palmatum*) stands to the right of the entrance. Opposite: Variegated hosta and a dwarf cutleaf birch (*Betula pendula* 'Trost's Dwarf') dominate the left side of the entrance near the sidewalk, with silver-gray lamb's ears (*Stachys byzantina*) and two wormwoods (*Artemisia*) on the right.

pathway to the door. Neither Peter nor I wanted a straight approach to the house."

At the time Judith was involved in growing her own herbs, and particularly liked the illustrations for classic herb gardens in one of her books. A round garden plan became the inspiration for the raised center bed surrounded by a path of granite setts (small, uniformly shaped chunks of granite often used as cobblestones years ago). Limestone boulders are embedded in its 2-foot depth of soil to retain it, although they're now nearly hidden by plants. More limestone boulders edge the entrance to the garden, all carefully placed by Peter. "He has a feeling for stone," Judith says. "He knows which sides to place together, and which sides should face out."

'Nice Gal' peony looks like a giant dahlia, blooms prolifically and never flops over, even without staking. Beside the peony, magenta cranesbill (*Geranium*) and a tall, silver-gray wormwood (*Artemisia*).

They'd rescued a few plants from the original foundation planting, including a lovely spirea, and the Japanese maple by the front door has been there from the beginning. "Once we had a big blue spruce by the end of the driveway (to the right of the front door), but the day it got so big we couldn't see the street until we'd completely backed out onto it, we said oops, it'll have to go." Judith says. The garden is freshened and updated every couple of years, with spent plants removed and replaced and overgrown plants pruned. The Adams did some major work about four years ago, the year of the disappearing maple, and it's remained pretty much the same since. A weeping caragana is a feature of the center circle bed, and a dappled willow standard grows near the bay window. "Normally the willow is a shrub that takes up all your precious space, but I prefer it as a standard because you can plant under it," Judith says. "Still, I have to prune it back two or three times a year."

Her color palette for the garden is muted, with many shades of rose and pink, a few blue blooms and lots of greens and textures. One side of the garden, to the right of the pathway as you face the house, tends to blues and grays, such as the lamb's ears and artemisia near the front sidewalk; the other moves into lighter greens and chartreuse, with plants like variegated 'June' hosta and a 'Trost's Dwarf' cutleaf birch. One of the features of the driveway side of the garden is the spectacular 'Nice Gal' peony, a cultivar that in Judith's experience never grows floppy and too tall, and never needs staking, and she doesn't understand why it's not more available in nurseries. "It's a magnet for the Oriental people in the neighborhood," Judith says. "They just love it, they come by and remark on it to each other, and they never look at anything else in the garden."

That's not like most people who pass by. They stop and admire the view, and many even take a stroll on the granite pathway circling the center bed. "I think front gardens should be made for your neighbors, and I make an effort to put nice plants in there that will beckon people in," Judith says. "The back garden can be for yourself." ■

Restoration Garden

IT'S NO WONDER the hard surfaces of Tammy and Rowan Sage's downtown garden have the patina of age, even though the garden itself is only six years old: the red clay bricks for the pathway were collected from the ruins of the city's ancient stockyard when it was torn down to make way for a huge shopping mall, and many of the stones supporting the raised beds came from the basement of a 1920s home on the next street, which was undergoing renovations. "We also picked up some limestone trimmings from a subway reconstruction site near us," says Tammy. "And a group of us on the street scooped up some nice old plants from the gardens of a couple of lovely old homes being torn down for new townhouses." But the rest of the garden, designed and installed by Tammy, is new, including her favorite golden chain tree and the deep pink lupines.

The porch and entrance are almost hidden by Tammy Sage's colorful late-spring garden. Golden chain tree (*Laburnum anagyroides*) takes center stage, and growing around it are rose and purple lupines (*Lupinus*). White bleeding heart (*Dicentra spectabilis* 'Alba') recedes into the background.

The garden has a simple but effective design, with a curved pathway that gives the 17-by-15-foot lot a sense of space because it nearly hides the steps to the porch as it disappears behind the central planting. After the spring bloom shown here is over, yellow, white and red daisies and blue campanula take over.

Tammy and Rowan, both botanists, are no strangers to plants and truly appreciate the enjoyment their small garden gives them. "It's so nice to come home at night and just look at plants and enjoy them, not to have to take them apart and analyze them," Tammy says. ■

Teresa Weindl's garden has an otherworldly quality lent it by the tall semi-tropical plants she moves outdoors every spring. Above: Tree fern (*Cyathea arborea*) seen in the center, schefflera (*Schefflera actinophylla*), right rear, and corn plant (*Zea mays*), foreground, are joined by less exotic but hardy shasta daisies (*Leucanthemum* x *superbum*), blue sage (*Salvia superba*, sometimes listed as *S. nemorosa* hybrids) and white hydrangea (*Hydrangea arborescens*). Below: The triffids along the porch railing were made by Teresa from discarded rakeheads and painted branches.

Urban Fantasy

Hamilton, Ontario

A BARELY NOTICEABLE sign outside Teresa Weindl's front door says Xanadu, and it's understandable that one assumes it refers to the garden, for it is indeed a magical, even fantastic, place. But in fact Xanadu is the name of the daycare center she operates from her house.

And from her garden too, of course. Kids and plants alike love Teresa's fanciful garden, which fills the 40-by-16-foot lot spanning both sides of the semi-detached house (Teresa's son occupies the other half). When she bought the century-old building fifteen years ago, the front yard was a dead zone of pavement where cars were parked, accessorized with rubble. Underneath the mess was arid, compacted soil. Over the years Teresa – a non-gardener up to that point, "although my mother was avid about it, so I guess I must have picked up something" – has turned it into a stop-and-stare destination on her street.

During the summer the garden bursts with lush rain-forest plants spending the summer outdoors and practical vegetables in large containers, as well as perennials such as iris, daylilies, hydrangeas, gladioli and chrysanthemums, plus hostas, ferns and vines for shades of green. Squeezed into every remaining corner are annuals: petunias, geraniums, begonias.

Impossible to overlook are the garden ornaments, all made by Teresa from bits and pieces she picks up here and there, sometimes with the "assistance" of the chidden. The

triffid-like flowers growing outside the porch railing are worn-out rake heads rescued from a local cemetery and mounted on painted twigs; the mobile hanging from the porch roof is made with discarded kitchen implements. A dream catcher lookalike by the front door is made of the business end of old tennis racquets, chicken wire and black silk ribbon.

Teresa admits she breaks the rules and allows her imagination to rule. But she also has a practical nature. "I like to move things around, so that's why I put things in planters," she says. "Besides, I have a small space and nearly every inch has a plant, but with containers I can always squeeze in just one more."

Her practical, even frugal, streak also induces her to bring annuals indoors to provide winter bloom. "There's no mystery to getting plants like impatiens to flower inside," she says. In late summer she chooses a day when indoor and outdoor temperatures are about the same, and simply brings the pots inside, making sure they've been liberally sprayed with insecticidal soap. "The hibiscus always has spider mites, so it has to be isolated." The plants are

Children who attend Teresa's daycare often eat lunch or do craft projects at the table in the rustic front-garden swing. The plastic flowers in the garden were made from metal rods and old packing materials, and are joined by real-life white-flowering hostas, hydrangeas and impatiens.

kept under lights or in a south window, fertilized regularly and cut back in late winter to produce new growth for the spring, when they go outside again.

People always want to know how she keeps her nursery school charges from damaging the flowers. "I don't have to worry about them," Teresa says. "They're involved in the garden from the spring, when planting begins, and they all have their jobs to do. Working with the plants gives them a sense of respect for nature." ∎

Showstoppers

One plant can often make a small garden, even if only for a brief period. The Japanese wisteria (*Wisteria floribunda*), above, is a good example. In a good year its bloom and perfume can be so spectacular one could wish for nothing more. In May, the Eastern redbud (*Cercis canadensis*), above right, a small tree native to the Carolinian area of northeastern Canada and the United States, puts on an unparalleled spring show with deep pink blooms along the branches. The bloom is followed by heart-shaped bright green leaves in summer and golden-yellow leaves in fall, making it a tree for all seasons.

Color is Key

Opposite: The minuscule midtown Toronto garden in front of the house of Lorraine Johnson and Andrew Leyerle, this book's principal photographer, stands out in spring because of its strong primary colors. In summer and into the fall, the garden is chockablock with the white, blue and yellow blooms of native black snakeroot (*Cimicifuga racemosa*), white baneberry (*Actaea pachypoda*), small Solomon's seal (*Polygonatum biflorum*), bottlebrush grass (*Hystrix patula*) brown-eyed Susan (*Rudbeckia triloba*) and New England aster (*Aster novae-angliae*). Despite the dense planting it's a simple garden, as befits its size, with a few rocks placed to anchor the setting and a natural path of gravel that widens to form a small entrance area at the base of the front steps.

Strips

Above: Houses set extremely close to the street are common in older urban neighborhoods, but one doesn't have to settle for grass or a ground cover to provide a softening touch of green. Here the tiny gardens have been planned to echo the houses' styles. In Ottawa, a white stucco cottage (above right) with pale, green-gray trim has a garden of casual, mounding plants that flow over the sidewalk, accented with a few tall exclamation points of color in the pink foxglove (*Digitalis*) and purple delphinium. Shrubs mark the corners of the garden. A more sophisticated style is used for the mirror-image garden (above left) used on both sides of semi-detached houses on a busy Montreal street. The gardens are planted in raised boxes under the windows, and filled with a restrained palette of plants in indigo, gray and lime green. The green sweet potato vine (*Ipomoea batatus* 'Marguerita') tumbles gracefully to the sidewalk, followed closely by white bacopa in the corner boxes. White flowering tobacco (*Nicotiana sylvestris*) is planted near the entrances.

Postage Stamp

Left: Much of the architecture in downtown Montreal has a distinctively European air, with large two-family dwellings of beautiful gray stone, and iron staircases to the upper apartments. The front yards may have been deeper a century ago, but as city sidewalks encroached there is little space left for gardens. That doesn't deter the dedicated, however. The residents of the lower apartment of this handsome home reap the greatest benefits of the eye-level garden. It has a casual, fully planted style that mixes colors at random. The low iron fencing lends a slightly formal air, especially based with a solid row of variegated goutweed (*Aegopodium podagraria* 'Variegatum'), a ground cover most gardeners regret planting because it can be so invasive. The sidewalks here will keep it under control on one side, and let's presume the iron fence will do the same on the other.

A Garden in Miniature

Even a small garden can have a landscape, as this small Montreal garden proves. The owner has turned her patch of land into a stroll garden with a path of random flagstones that widens in one spot to create a sitting or viewing location. Except for the orange daylilies sprouting up behind the iron fence to the right of the entranceway, foreground plants are kept low so pedestrians can appreciate the colorful foundation planting as they pass by. The mosaic of ground covers is the garden's standout feature, with the golden creeping Jenny (*Lysimachia nummularia* 'Aurea') and pansies a study in contrasts complemented by pink miniature roses and 'White Clips' campanula (*Campanula carpatica* 'White Clips'). The house is the perfect subdued yet classy background – handsome gray stone with black trim, and matching lace curtains at window and door.

Creating a Small Garden

The first and last rule about designing a small garden is this: keep it simple, my friend. Decide on one use or style and stay the course.

Before you put in even one plant or place a single ornament, look hard at the space. Measure it – you might find it's no bigger than the smallest bedroom in your house, or as large as your living room. It's often hard for the eye to grasp the potential of empty space, so it helps to have actual dimensions and something to compare them to. Thinking of it as a room often helps define the space and its style.

Consider what style will suit your house, remembering that every decorative element and every plant shows in a small garden, especially when it's close to the street. Maintain continuity with the details of the house: a white picket fence on a formal stone townhouse would be out of place, but the black painted iron fences, doors and window trim on pages 86 and 88 are examples of how to do it right. These are almost subliminal influences, but the eye records the similarities or the differences even if the mind doesn't make a conscious connection. Your neighborhood counts, too: every one has its own subtle identity, and you wouldn't want to deviate too far from the acceptable, even if you are a dedicated individualist.

And as you would do with any garden, look at the conditions of shade, sun, soil and moisture, plus the effects of street traffic if you're in the city. This will affect what kinds of plants you can grow successfully. And definitely consider enriching or replacing the soil before you begin – lots of plants in a small space deserve all the help they can get.

Here are some ideas to inspire you:

- Are **vegetables** or herbs your heart's desire? A lovely four-square potager centered with a sun dial will bring compliments in a sophisticated urban setting, even if you've included a couple of sprawling tomato plants.

- A scrupulously tended miniature **market garden** done in rows, with colorful ornamental veggies like ruby Swiss chard (*Beta vulgaris* 'Ruby Red'), 'Giulio' radicchio (*Chicorium intybus* 'Giulio'), bright green leaf lettuce and the architectural stems of garlic, will look interesting and different.

- Something **formal**? Plan a symmetrical garden in a simple palette of no more than three colors complemented with lots of greens.

- Definitely **modern**? Floor it with a Bauhausian combination of blocks of slate and stone aggregate outlined in low santolinas (*Santolina chamaecyparissus*) or edged with a dense growth of hens and chicks (*Sempervivum*). Leave some blocks open to hold strong foliage plants, such as hosta, yucca or grasses.

- Must have a **prairie**? Definitely think small here, although it's possible to grow one in miniature. Stick to a few plants in large drifts, which will give the garden its structure. Choose short grasses and low prairie plants, lovely things like shooting star (*Dodecatheon meadia*, or *D. hendersonii*) and prairie crocus (*Pulsatilla vulgaris*) for spring, prairie smoke (*Geum triflorum*) for summer, plus prairie dropseed (*Sporobolus heterolepsis*) or the more cultivated blue fescue grass (*Festuca glauca*). And include a small access path.

- Thinking **Oriental**? Small gardens lend themselves well to restrained Chinese or Japanese styles. Concentrate on simplicity and tranquility, and include gravel, a few large boulders, a couple of ground covers and a stand of bamboo – or caragana (*Caragana arborescens*) pruned as upright stems, bamboo style.

Structure

In formal gardens the structure is obvious, but informal gardens need structure, too. Create a framework with a strong pathway, as Tammy Sage did in her garden (page 81). Use a low hedge of clipped boxwood or miniature roses to define and contain flower beds.

Manipulate your space. You can add a sense of mystery to a long, narrow garden – plus fool the eye into thinking it's bigger than it is – by using a curving path to divide the space. Use an "S" shape if you can, with a planting of perennials or low shrubs at one of the curves to hide what's beyond. The eye will assume there's more yard than there is. A modified "C" works in a shorter space: from the house, curve the path around the perimeter of the garden and back to a small pond in the corner.

Shallow gardens look longer with design lines running from the house to the street: use an *allée* of small trees, a low hedge or even a path that narrows slightly toward the back.

In a really tiny garden, use a thin but attractive structure, such as a lattice or bamboo screen (or, if you're artistic, a fence with a *trompe l'oeil* design), to separate a section from the rest of the space. It may only hide the composter or other garden equipment, but it will give a sense that the garden holds more than it does.

If you have a slope, even a shallow one, don't wail over it – capitalize on it.

Cut into the slope and create a step down from the upper area to the lower with a retaining wall of flat stones. Plant creeping ground covers below and mounding plants that will spill over the stone above. Make the slope deeper and more dramatic by raising the upper level with extra soil.

Focal points

Stick to one. Get rid of superfluous objects or design elements – for example, don't even think of using both a bench and a fountain. The secret is not to confuse or overcrowd the space.

Small accessories – even if used in a group – make a small garden look fussy and meager. Choose single

Formal's the Word

Only the tall evergreen deviates from the formal balance of this downtown Toronto garden, and it serves to add variety to the repeating pattern of the smaller shrubs. The garden picks up on the essentially formal pattern of the street and acts as a transition to a relatively formal house. A low iron fence (the top is just visible in the foreground) encloses the garden, which is bordered with a squared-off boxwood hedge. But rounded forms predominate, including the center circle of paving stones holding an urn filled with pink ivy geraniums and trailing white bacopa (*Sutera cordata*). The small-leaved evergreens were carefully chosen to provide a variety of textures and shades of green. Apart from careful pruning two or three times a year, the garden is low maintenance.

items that reveal your confidence in the attractiveness of your garden, and extend this philosophy to hard surfaces like large paving stones, substantial fence finials and wide steps.

View a really tiny space as a stage set and dress it accordingly. For example, you could develop a Mediterranean theme in an 8-by-8-foot space by setting one tall, empty (it's more dramatic that way) terra-cotta urn in the center of a bed of gravel and surrounding it with creeping thymes or other low herbs. It will make a strong, simple statement.

Use a screen or arbor as your one focal point. An arbor smothered in roses can lead the visitor into your garden from the street or the driveway, or point the way to the back garden, and provide the garden's architectural element as well. A lattice screen placed on the lot line between your house and your neighbor's, covered with clematis or another delicate vine, can create a non-threatening wall that separates the two spaces and gives the eye something to focus on.

Reverse the formula and create a focal point that's viewed from the house, not just by passersby: frame a bench, a pond or a bird bath at the street end of your garden, facing the house, with a wide, strong arbor covered with wisteria. A more delicate look can be achieved with an arbor of copper tubing and clematis, jasmine or annual morning glory.

Instead of an arbor or arch, use freestanding wood or metal obelisks, hollow pillars made of trelliswork and capped with molding, or bamboo canes lashed together wigwam style as the focal piece of your garden.

Water

Water features are popular in backyard gardens, why not in the front, too? One immense shallow pot filled with water and a few largish boulders and set in a bed of river stones makes an attractive focus for a foliage garden.

A tall chimney pot or large-size weeping tile makes a good stand for a small pond form. Set it into the top and add a small fountain or cascade, hiding the wiring for the submersible pump in the base.

Formal pond edges are easier to deal with than the informal, Mother-Nature-must-have-made-it kind. It's easy to install a large pond in the center of your small front garden with a simple fiberglass form set flush in the ground and surrounded with slabs of stone. Grow a low, clipped hedge, lavender or other slow-growing, easy-to-trim herb around it.

For the easiest approach of all don't bother with a fountain, which will require an electrical source to power a submersible water pump; make it a still pond filled with water lilies. In a small garden make water the focus, instead of just part of the design: design a shallow square or rectangular pond that almost fills the space, outline it with paving stones or brick that overhang the edge, and install stepping stones or small bridges in or over the water so you can walk through it.

Plants

Choose plants for a small garden carefully. Try to find shrubs and small trees that offer something of value in more than one season – the ideal would be flowers in spring, shapely foliage in summer that takes on color in fall, and berries for birds in winter. But two out of four is good. All your plants should have good foliage and form, especially trees and shrubs that lose their leaves in winter. Don't settle for plants that don't instantly attract you with their beauty.

Allow plants enough room to mature to their regular size. Most important, don't buy varieties that will eventually take over the whole garden – stick to dwarf varieties. However, one striking medium-size specimen tree, such as a Japanese maple or a redbud, or even a gnarled lilac or crab apple, adds personality and presence to a small space. This goes for perennials like hosta, too: one huge perennial can be your garden's focal point, although it's summertime event only, without a winter presence. Try *Hosta* 'Krossa Regal', *H. sieboldiana* 'Elegans' or *H.* 'Sum and Substance'.

A dwarf Alberta spruce (*Picea glauca* 'Conica') fits well in a tiny Toronto garden. In front, the foliage of variegated iris and *Sedum acre* blend with yellow daylilies.

Perennials

An important resource is your local nursery's horticulturist, who can help you choose the right varieties of your favorite plants for a small garden in your growing zone.

Choose cultivars of native plants, which usually bloom longer than the species, such as *Monarda* 'Marshall's Delight' and *Echinacea purpurea* 'Magnus'. Seek out long-blooming cultivars of other plants, such as *Rosa* 'The Fairy' or the 'Bonica' rose, which flower from July to frost in most areas. *Hemerocallis* 'Stella de Oro' is a dependable, cheery daylily that blooms almost all summer. It's low growing, too.

Avoid spreaders like white gooseneck loosestrife (*Lysimachia clethroides*) and obedient plant (*Physostegia virginiana*) – they like to be boss. Look for dwarf varieties of perennials, such as: 'Rubra' masterwort (*Astrantia carniolica* 'Rubra'); *Astilbe* 'Sprite' or *Astilbe chinensis* 'Pumila'; *Hosta sieboldii* 'Kabitan', with narrow yellow slightly ruffled leaves; lady's mantle (*Alchemilla alpina* or *Alchemilla ellenbeckii*, which grow to a height of about 6 and 4 inches respectively).

Annuals

Use them sparingly because they won't give you winter interest and you don't want them to overwhelm your garden, but definitely use them. Choose annuals that give you a bang for your buck – bright orange-yellow California poppies (*Eschscholzia californica*) are great, although they do reseed and have to be edited out the next spring. They look terrific with the foot-tall spires of the better-behaved mealycup sage (*Salvia farinacea* 'Blue Victory'). More showy choices are Australian fan flower (*Scaevola aemula*), verbena and *Calibrachoa*, the small petunia lookalike also sold as Million Bells. Icicle series pansies (*Viola x wittrockiana*) are miraculous – they start blooming in fall and often last right through winter and pick up again in spring.

Chapter Seven

Opulent Gardens

To beginners, a successful garden usually means flowers, lots of them, blooming non-stop for the entire growing season. Experienced gardeners, however, know that

learning how to do this can take a lifetime of trying, and then you run out of time. This is just a fact of life, not meant to discourage anyone – as all true gardeners know, it's the journey that's important, not the destination.

Modern flower gardens have a history that goes back to the Victorians. Eugène Chevreul's theory of complementary color, which he developed as a chemist for the Gobelin tapestry works in England, influenced the Victorians' obsession for highly charged color and intricate pattern. The Victorians fell in love with vivid patterned carpet beds planted like jewels, and their love of opulence influenced the gardening world till the late nineteenth century, when the more subtle color and planting theories of Gertrude Jekyll and Claude Monet gained favor.

Jekyll, a plantswoman with a background in art, specialized in long borders of perennials and shrubs planted in drifts of changing color, usually pastels, although she sometimes used hot colors tempered with gray. Monet planted as he painted, with an Impressionist's eye for soft, blending colors that blur into patterns of light and shade. Both gardened on a scale we can only wish for, but their Impressionistic approach to flower gardens remains with us today. The gardens in this chapter represent the most successful among us, people who garden freely and opulently, with the artist's eye for combining color and massing plants, while maintaining a sense of order in the garden.

In opulent gardens, flowers fill almost every square inch of space. Opposite: Long-blooming roses such as 'The Fairy' carry this garden through the season, with Asiatic lilies and blue delphiniums dropping in for a midsummer show. Above: Roses, sweet alyssum (*Lobularia maritima*) and lady's mantle (*Alchemilla mollis*) spill over the pathway.

"I'M AN EXHIBITIONIST, I admit it," says Dianne Dietrich, with a peal of infectious laughter. "And I have a front garden because it's a great way to get lots of attention." This may stretch the truth a bit. The fact is that Dianne is an obsessive gardener who can't bear to see earth go to waste, and she can't abide large expanses of lawn. "Huge lawns with shrubs and one maple tree in the front were the norm where I grew up, except for our place," she says. "My dad had an exuberant front garden, with coral bells, begonias, jack-in-the-pulpit, campanula, herbs, everything. My parents really set a standard for me."

The cascades of plants tumbling over the fence and onto the sidewalk in her own exuberant garden invite people to come in and explore. "I made a decision when I moved in here that I would start a front garden right away," Dianne says. "In my old place I didn't do the front at first, but once I did I realized people appreciated it. They'd stop to talk and share ideas, and even if we never met they got to know my plants."

She tells about a man she met for the first time at a neighborhood party, a non-gardener who nevertheless was an admirer of several of her garden's treasures, including a tiny blue and yellow 'George' early spring iris he enthused about over drinks. "That little iris gave him so much pleasure," she says. "I planted about a hundred more that fall, just for him."

Her front garden, says Dianne, is her signature. "Front gardens should be unique, and different from back gardens, which are by nature elitist because you have to be invited in to see them," she says. "A front garden is generous – it's part of the community and it should help set a standard for gardening in the neighborhood."

Dianne Dietrich's exuberant garden boasts a split-rail fence made by Dianne and an ancient iron maple syrup cauldron, just one of many found objects she's picked up on her travels. Her color sensibility shows up in the purple and blue color scheme of this portion of the early summer garden: Japanese maple (*Acer palmatum*), iris (*Iris germanica*) and alliums.

An Exuberant Garden

Toronto, Ontario

When she moved into her 1930s home on a pleasant old Toronto street in the mid-1990s, the front hardly set a standard of design. The remnants of a border garden were vaguely visible – a few alliums, a lilac, an old rose, globe thistles and lilies. Dianne kept some of the original plants in honor of the old garden, but otherwise the property is unrecognizable. It's thick with plants: simple, old-fashioned ones such as phlox and clematis, iris and artemisia, but with many of them in new hybrid forms. The concrete-pad sidewalk that once led from the street directly to the front door has been replaced by staggered flagstones surrounded by sprawling ground covers. A small pond is tucked into a space near the pathway. Tall poles hold aloft birdhouses and support an ancient street sign found in an antiques market, wind chimes sing in the breeze and ornamental grasses wave gracefully.

"In the front, the plants, the design elements and the house should have some kind of congruity," says Dianne. The split-rail fence (which Dianne built herself) across the front and up one side of her house is an example. It has a country air that befits her farmhouse-style home. "It's also a creative vehicle for growing plants against, and it's a bit of a barrier for kids, although I love having them come in to see the garden. I'm sure I confuse those poor kids – sometimes I'm the wicked witch of the west but other times I'm some kind of benevolent earth mother, depending on

what they're doing and what's happening in the garden."

Dianne says her front garden is especially important because it's the essential view from the house, winter and summer. The kitchen of the open-plan interior is oriented toward the street, and its center of operations is a large harvest table where she does everything – even potting up plants in spring. From the table she can watch the birds pulling out the zebra grass and the fluffy seedheads of golden clematis for their nests. "Its little yellow flowers aren't my favorite, but I'd never get rid of that plant because the birds love it so much," she says.

For February bloom she's planted 'Jelena', her favorite witch hazel, by the door of the small unheated front porch, and under it some winter aconite, a plant she considers underrated. "They give you so much with their collars of

Dianne is a natural at combining plant textures and colors.

Opposite top: The fluffy seedheads of golden clematis (*Clematis tangutica*) contrast with spiky zebra grass (*Miscanthus sinensis* 'Zebrinus') and soft, gray-green artemisia. The same plants show in a view inside the garden (opposite bottom), along with a tall orange yarrow (*Achillea millefolium* 'Paprika').

Above: The large, leathery leaves of *Bergenia cordifolia* and strong variegated foliage of 'Patriot' hosta are also part of the combination. A small pond, right, nearly covered with fairy moss (*Azolla*) and bordered with Japanese maple and a purple clematis, is hidden in the planting.

Dianne makes good use of found objects such as the bamboo wind chimes, above, in her garden. The low seat beside the pond, below, is a slice rescued from the dangerously leaning Manitoba maple that had to be cut down beside the house. Hugging the pond seat: a dwarf magenta geranium (*Geranium cinereum* 'Ballerina'). On the left is orange yarrow (*Achillea millefolium* 'Paprika') and feathery variegated reed grass (*Calamagrostis acutifolia* 'Overdam').

foliage and those pretty yellow flowers." Under the lilac she has 'White Nancy' lamium, loads of 'Prince Klaus' crocus and purple and white pansies, which she plants in fall so she'll get early bloom. These groupings she can appreciate as she comes and goes from the house.

What she originally saw from her kitchen window was a dangerously leaning Manitoba maple she decided had to come down. To kill it, her brother ringed the tree by cutting around the trunk to a depth of about an inch, which prevents the sap from reaching the branches. A few weeks later Dianne woke up in the middle of the night feeling badly about what she'd done. In the morning she phoned tree experts to find out how to save the tree. "Nothing, they said. It's gone. I looked at the birds in the tree and felt terrible." But the next spring the tree bounced back in full leaf, with not a symptom of trouble.

Dianne felt relief, but soon changed her mind again. The tree was leaning dangerously, and besides, she wanted a sunnier garden. So she made a plan: the tree would be cut off at exactly the right height – 4 feet, 3 inches – to hold a planter that would provide the perfect view from the kitchen window. She hired a tree removal expert who did the job exactly as ordered. "Then a neighbor came by, upset because I'd cut down a tree, and I felt bad all over again," she laughs. "What do you do?"

Today the stump supports a large iron maple syrup cauldron filled with plants, lifted there with the help of several friends. True to Dianne's frugal nature, the rest of the tree has been recycled in many ways. Part of it has been cut into planks that serve as stairs in the back garden, and a thick slice of the trunk is a seat in the garden. ■

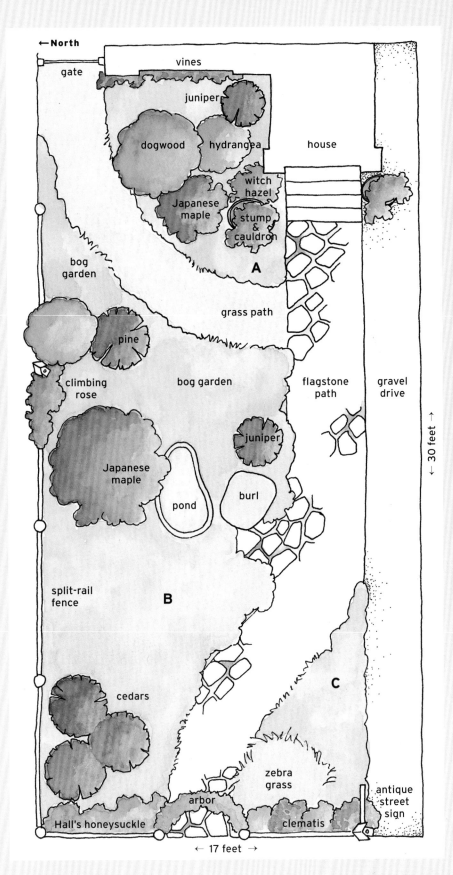

Garden Plan

Bog gardens ligularia, monkshood, primrose, pasqueflower, hosta, meadowsweet, iris, daylily, black mondo grass, shooting star, lamb's ears, lamium

A lilies, daylily, coreopsis, yarrow, cushion spurge, salvia, hens and chicks, artemisia, white coneflower, knotweed, tall and dwarf iris, all underplanted with spring bulbs and pansies

B perennial geranium, allium, monkshood, tall and dwarf iris, artemisia, coral bells, bronze fennel, salvia, columbine, globe thistle, woodland phlox, bergenia, yarrow, cushion spurge, ornamental grasses, clematis, Culver's root, sea lavender

C ornamental grasses, aster, allium, salvia, lavender, artemisia, iris, cushion spurge

Labels within plan:
← North
gate
vines
juniper
dogwood
hydrangea
house
witch hazel
Japanese maple
stump & cauldron
A
bog garden
grass path
pine
climbing rose
bog garden
flagstone path
gravel drive
juniper
Japanese maple
burl
pond
← 30 feet →
split-rail fence
B
cedars
C
zebra grass
arbor
antique street sign
Hall's honeysuckle
clematis
← 17 feet →

ONE DAY WHEN Dorothy Durdos was having her nails done at a local salon, she fell into conversation with the woman at the next table, who was a real-estate agent. "So do you live anywhere near that house with the picket fence and all the flowers in front?" asked the woman, trying to establish Dorothy's domain.

"Well, yes," said Dorothy. "That's my house."

The real estate agent's jaw dropped. That's not an uncommon reaction among people who drive along the street where Dorothy lives with her husband, Julio, when the garden comes into view. On a street of barren new homes with large garages in front and great expanses of asphalt road designed to move as much traffic as quickly as possible, the Durdos garden is a landmark, a point of reference, an incredible oasis of pink and white roses, blue delphinium, yellow lilies and more.

Even children watch for it. "People have told me their kids keep an eye out as they're driving along and yell out 'Mommy, mommy, there's the garden!'" says Dorothy. "Then they all have to stop and look at it. I find that very rewarding."

Perhaps more rewarding was the appreciation of an elderly English woman who walked by the garden with her daughter several times a week one summer. "She clearly had Alzheimer's," says Dorothy, a nurse who manages a home for the aged, "and she always said 'Here's the English garden' and stepped inside the gate to stand for a while and smell the flowers. I think it gave her some pleasure."

The perfume inside the gate is almost overwhelming, a heady mixture (depending on the season) of roses, petunias, lilies, magnolia, crab apple and cherry blossoms. The

Dorothy and Julio Durdos' garden is a flowery beacon on their otherwise stark street of asphalt, concrete and grass. People stop to admire the profusion of roses, mainly long-blooming varieties like pale-pink 'The Fairy', in the foreground with deep-pink petunias. The entrance patio is a fragrant place to sit on summer evenings.

An English Garden
Mississauga, Ontario

white picket fence, which Dorothy copied from one she saw in a magazine, comes in for its share of admiration, too. One summer a woman from Cape Cod asked if she could photograph it so she could build one like it for her garden. Dorothy was flattered. "Here was this woman from a place where they have some of the loveliest gardens in the United States and she wanted my fence!" she says.

But all this attention can have its drawbacks, Dorothy admits. "I love people stopping to talk, and we meet some really interesting ones, but it's hard to get the weeding done," she says. "So now Julio and I go out early in the morning to do the important chores and leave the easy stuff for later in the day."

They moved into their new home in the summer of 1995, and immediately Dorothy decided she had to do something about the angular appearance of the house. "I've always felt that front yards are the most underused space," she says. "In the suburbs especially people spend all their time in the back and ignore the possibilities of the front. Our neighborhood looked so cold and naked. I thought a garden would give our house some personality."

It was the garden in the magazine that initially inspired her. In the article, the fence's owner said her front garden had brought her in touch with her neighborhood. There was lots of pedestrian traffic on her street, Dorothy observed, but she never got to meet the people, so maybe a front garden would be the answer.

The first thing she planted was a magnolia tree. "I had to have one. I grew up in Ottawa where they aren't hardy, but I knew it would be fine here, in that little protected courtyard up near the house," she says. Then a flowering crab went in, and a Japanese cherry beside the garage. "I just wanted a garden with a lot of flowers. That's why I decided on an English garden, with lots of roses."

It had to be a low-maintenance rose garden, although that thought will make most gardeners smile. But Dorothy consulted with a nursery that specializes in roses and came up with a workable plan: lots of 'Bonica' inside the fence;

'The Fairy' outside the fence; and low-growing Flower Carpet series roses (a group of small, flowered spreading plants available in apple blossom pink, rose pink, coral and white) next to the driveway. None of these varieties need coddling and, better yet, they bloom from July to October. In Dorothy's garden they're augmented through the season by blue delphiniums, lilies, hosta and annuals to fill any remaining spaces.

A small patch of grass remains just inside the fence. Dorothy and Julio have talked about taking out the grass and putting in more roses. "But I worry about the robins," Dorothy says. "We have several families nesting in our trees, and they pull worms out of the grass to feed the babies. I couldn't take that away from them." Naturally, pesticides are never used on the plants, for the robins' sake and because of the couple's general philosophy about avoiding poisonous substances in the garden. "I spray with insecticidal soap and I use a solution of baking soda and water for fungus diseases," Dorothy says.

A couple of changes have been made since the garden was put in, and Dorothy wonders why they didn't think of them before they dug the first shovelful of earth: garden lighting and an underground sprinkler system. "So we called some guys and explained what we wanted," Dorothy says. "They took one look at all the gardens and the big stone courtyard by the front door, then said 'Yeah, right.' But they did it, and so well they didn't disturb a plant. Now the roses get a good soaking automatically, and the water doesn't flood the foliage, which would be bad for them."

Dorothy gardens just as obsessively in the back, where she grows hybrid tea roses, Austins, floribundas and Explorers, and comes by her avocation honestly. "My family had a cattle farm, and both my Mom and my grandmother were big gardeners," she says. When the farm was sold she transplanted a huge Japanese peony, pink chrysanthemums, several other plants and a statue of a cow, all of which grace her back garden. "My Mom thinks I have too many flowers in the front," says Dorothy. "Do you think she might be jealous?" ■

Dorothy has added many plants seen in English-style gardens to the roses she favors. Below: Yellow Asiatic lilies, purple-blue delphiniums and a pale-pink hydrangea. Opposite: A small patch of grass remains inside the fence because it supplies worms to the robins nesting in the garden's trees. Foreground: a rose-pink Flower Carpet rose.

A Blowsy Welcome

The house is used as a backdrop for the blowsy Vancouver garden opposite, and its stucco and stone exterior blends perfectly with the English-style garden. Shrubs and taller plants such as *Verbena bonariensis*, shrub roses and Japanese anemone (*Anemone hybrida*) are kept toward the middle and rear of the garden, with lower, mounding plants like annual sweet alyssum (*Lobularia maritima*) in the foreground. All are in muted tones of pink and red softened with white. Even the plants tumbling over the pathway add to the subtle welcoming effect.

Simply Productive

Self-seeding annuals and vegetable plants play an important role in the simple, unplanned Thunder Bay, Ontario, garden above. The pink and red opium poppies (*Papaver somniferum*) along the sidewalk put on a good show in summer, but die back in August, leaving rather tattered foliage and gorgeous beige seedpods. The plants pop up in greater numbers every year and will take over the garden unless some of them are prevented from setting seed. Potatoes grow beside the driveway in a full-sun bed, and dependable orange daylilies (*Hemerocallis*), pale mauve phlox and rosy-pink achillea form the backbone of the perennial garden in summer.

Creating an Opulent Garden

Most front gardens just grow, expanding from the house to the street as the gardener digs up more and more of the grass. While a plan of some kind is always a good idea, it's especially important if you're developing a garden filled with flowers. For the sake of the neighborhood and your own reputation, you don't want your garden to look overgrown and out of control by mid-summer. Nor do you want it looking sad and barren in winter, showing nothing but earth and dead perennial tops. Perhaps more than any other style, opulent, flowery gardens require good planning, both in structure and plantings. Don't even think of starting till you have some idea of where you're heading – Mother Nature may be able to wing it, but most mere mortals can't.

Paths

Pathways are essential in opulent gardens. You need at least one to wind through the plantings and provide access for weeding and deadheading. A geometric path, in a cruciform or X pattern, automatically creates a more formal structure. But keep paths narrow – in other parts of the garden they should be wide enough for two people, but in a flowery front yard garden a wide path would dominate. Two feet should be enough to allow plants to grow over the edges and allow the gardener to pass through, although it may not leave room for a wheelbarrow.

Hedges and Fences

A low hedge – of boxwood (*Buxus*), clipped rosemary, southernwood (*Artemisia abrotanum*) or other compact foliage plant – can also create structure in a blowsy garden. In my back garden a half circle of boxwood beside the gravel path running behind our house contains low ground covers that can be seen through the French doors of the living room. The hedge holds back taller plants, which grow outside the semi-circle and would love to invade it. Split-rail or picket fences within a garden also provide structure and definition to the plantings.

Focal points

Small ponds, statuary and arbors can be used to separate plants and create order in opulent gardens. See the pictures on pages 96 and 97 to learn how one of our gardeners used a tree stump and a small pond with an adjoining sitting spot to provide shape and discipline to her flower-filled garden.

Color

Like music and scent, color can affect moods, and many gardeners subconsciously choose plants in colors that make them feel good. But low-key or simple is usually more effective than an eye-popping swath of hot color, even if your favorite colors are orange and red. A restricted palette of varying harmonies of one shade maintains its appeal for years, especially in a small garden. In a large garden you could adapt Gertrude Jekyll's "rainbow" approach to borders by planting large areas of many single colors and blending them together as in a rainbow.

But gardens never stay static, and your most careful color scheme will shift from year to year as the garden evolves and the weather affects blooming times. There's also something to be said for experimenting – go ahead and plant those orange poppies next to the red dahlias if you like. They may look stunning, and no one says you can't take them out if you tire of the combination.

Color Guidelines

- Pale colors stand out in the shade and in the evening.
- Colors are their purest and brightest in the clear light of spring. This is when pale colors shine in the garden.
- Bright, hot colors tend to fade in the bright sun of summer, and yellow becomes almost blinding. Rich, deep colors are best for this season.
- The more golden, weaker light of fall complements strong colors that might look gaudy in summer. Oranges, yellows and bronze look good in the season's mellow light.
- Colors affect each other – for example, a blue that's cool and restful on its own can take on a mauve tone and become moody next to a clear red, which becomes more crimson beside the blue. But a touch of white nearby returns them to normal.
- Blues cool all colors and suggest distance. Plant blue flowers at the end of the garden to give the impression of depth.
- Reds add drama and excitement to a planting. Use it in moderation unless you're striving for an effect. Play it down by combining with blues or deep purple.
- Yellows should be used carefully or they can take on a brassy personality. The pale tones are the sweetest and work well in a pastel garden. All yellows look good with tones of blue.

Top: White tuberous begonias with blue ageratum (*Ageratum houstonianum*) and pink impatiens. Middle top: Purple coneflower (*Echinacea purpurea*), wild bee balm (*Monarda fistulosa*) and false sunflower (*Heliopsis helianthoides*). Middle bottom: Rose, pansies and sweet alyssum (*Lobularia maritima*). Bottom: Rhododendron, Japanese maple (*Acer palmatum*) and coral bells (*Heuchera*).

Plants

Planting Style

Use plants to create pattern and cohesion in the garden. A drift or sweep of one plant leads the eye to the next grouping, or around the corner of the house, inviting the viewer to explore the rear garden.

The kaleidoscope effect, with single plants in many colors sprinkled throughout the garden, is tiring and busy and not usually the best way to display flowers. But it can be made to work if the colors are woven together with lots of white flowers and green foliage plants.

Fragrance

Plant a few varieties with perfume, especially to enjoy in the evening, when you're most likely to be sitting near your garden: white petunias, night-scented stock (*Matthiola longipetala* subsp. *bicornis*), flowering tobacco (*Nicotiana sylvestris*), moonflower vine (*Ipomoea alba*), brugmansia, and heliotrope. See page 205 for more suggestions.

Foliage

Choose plants with a variety of shapes and foliage textures. Combine rounded and upright shapes, and plants with spiky foliage and large round leaves. Foliage color is important, too: seek out grayish tones, bright and deep greens, plants with leaves that veer toward chartreuse and bluish tones. Color and texture in the foliage keep a garden interesting even when it's not in full bloom.

Purple smoke bush

Seasonal Interest

Plan for visual interest throughout the seasons. If you live in the north, include low evergreens or dwarf shrubs with architectural bark. Be sure you have low plants that retain foliage into the winter, such as thymes, wintergreen (*Gaultheria procumbens*), bearberry or kinnikinick (*Arctostaphylos uva-ursi*), cotoneaster (*Cotoneaster dammeri*) and periwinkle (*Vinca minor*), or those with interesting seedheads.

Use spring-flowering bulbs generously if you live in the north. They offer color in the garden from February or March through June, when the main perennials take over and annuals begin to come into their own.

Moss phlox and tulips

Spring

Bulbs

camassia (*Camassia leichtlinii, C. quamash*)

crocus (*Crocus*)

daffodil (*Narcissus*)

early spring iris (*Iris danfordiae, I. histroides, I. reticulata, I. bucharica*)

early to late tulips

fritillaria (*Fritillaria*)

glory of the snow (*Chionodoxa*)

mariposa lily (*Calochortus*)

scilla (*Scilla*)

shooting star (*Dodecatheon meadia*)

snowdrops (*Galanthus nivalis*)

trout lily (*Erythonium*)

winter aconite (*Eranthis hyemalis*)

Perennials

cushion spurge (*Euphorbia polychroma*)
foamflower (*Tiarella cordifolia*)
lenten rose (*Helleborus orientalis*)
lupine (*Lupinus*)
peony (*Paeonia*)
phlox (*Phlox subulata, P. divaricata, P. adsurgens, P. maculata*)
primrose (*Primula*)

Blue fan flower

Early to Mid-Summer

balloon flower (*Platycodon grandiflorus*)
bee balm (*Monarda didyma*)
big betony (*Stachys grandiflora*)
blanket flower (*Gaillardia*)
daylily (*Hemerocallis*)
delphinium (*Delphinium*)
foxtail lily (*Eremurus*)
gayfeather, blazing star (*Liatris spicata*)
Jacob's ladder (*Polemonium*)
Maltese cross (*Lychnis chalcedonica*)
pincushion flower (*Scabiosa columbaria* 'Butterfly Blue', 'Pink Mist')

roses of all kinds, particularly the Austin, Explorer, Parkland and Pavement series, plus polyantha, floribunda and grandiflora roses
shasta daisy (*Leucanthemum x superbum*)
spike speedwell (*Veronica spicata*)
Stokes' aster (*Stokesia laevis*)

Late Summer to Fall

African daisy (*Osteospermum*)
border phlox (*Phlox paniculata*)
canna (*Canna*)
chrysanthemum (*Chrysanthemum*)
goldenrod cultivars (*Solidago* cultivars)
'Goldsturm' rudbeckia (*Rudbeckia fulgida* 'Goldsturm')
ligularia (*Ligularia dentata* 'Othello', *L. dentata* 'Desdemona')
obedient plant (*Physostegia virginiana*)
purple coneflower (*Echinacea purpurea*)
purple-leaved fountain grass (*Pennisetum setaceum* 'Rubrum')
Russian sage (*Perovskia atriplicifolia*)
sedum (*Sedum spectabile*)

For all-season annuals to fill spaces between perennial blooming times, see Cottage Gardens, page 73.

New England asters, 'Autumn Joy' sedum, and fountain grass

Minimalist Gardens

Like a lot of design trends, minimalism began as a reaction to what came before, in this case the opulence and over-ornamentation of the Edwardian and Victorian

periods. In the early part of the twentieth century stream-lined art-deco styles had a brief say, then architects like Le Corbusier and Mies van de Rohe brought the concept of minimalism to the design of buildings and interiors, and the phrases "less is more" and "form follows function" entered our lexicon.

Naturally, these ideas seeped into garden design as the century developed. But minimalism in garden design was not new. The ancient gardens of Greece and Rome, the Mughal gardens of India and even the Aztec gardens of Montezuma were small, highly formalized private spaces devoted to the principles of minimalism. And for centuries Japanese gardens have been models of simple elegance, landscapes of nature in microcosm, with every stone or plant meriting its own special attention.

A garden that's pared down to its essential spirit has a peaceful, sometimes sophisticated quality, and long-time gardeners sated with beds billowing with plants often turn to the more orderly and simple. They appreciate foliage of varying textures and shades of green, the subtle beauty of rock or the stark architecture of a tree's limbs.

Minimalist gardens are especially appropriate with modern houses of the last half-century, especially structures whose ornamentation has been kept to the functional. A simple garden design and a restricted palette of plants are the general rule, perhaps combined with a specimen rock or a single piece of stunning sculpture.

Opposite: The hard landscaping around the garden matches the house in both design and materials. The concrete entrance pads reflect the home's square, masculine style, and the gravel mulch complements its color. The plants also have a strong presence: round pads of opuntia cactus play off the stark stems of the thorny ocotillo (*Fouquiera splendens*) in the background, and both are softened by mounding pink verbena, foreground. Above: In this northern minimalist garden, a crab apple tree adds a note of color in spring to the dry stream bed and the emerging plants.

GORDON WHITE'S gorgeous stone driveway is a work of art, and an important design element in his garden. He thinks of it as a mosaic, and he hasn't driven over it in more than two years. The two-car garage, built into one side of the clean-lined modern home, is now a storage area. And what about the car? "I leave it on the street," Gordon says.

Sometimes people reaching the end of his street insist on backing into his driveway to turn their vehicles around, but Gordon has found a deterrent. "I put a specimen stone there. It's only a small one, but it's big enough that drivers know when they graze it, even when they're in a big SUV," he says mischievously.

But Gordon White could never be mean. He just loves his driveway – indeed, his whole garden is his avocation (in his day job he's a neurosurgeon), and although he inherited a space with "good bones" when he bought the house in 1991, he's refined and softened the plan with care and much attention to design detail.

The house was built in the early 1980s on a piece of land separated from the property next door, a large home and grounds that dates back to the 1920s. The area originally housed a horse farm and stables, and Gordon's street was a bridle path, with a running track around the corner. It's a lovely space, with a city-owned ravine that carries off water from local creeks curving gently on the garage side of his lot, and many trees. "All the trees were preserved when this house was built," Gordon says. "It was sort of fitted into the lot."

In the old days the driveway, an asphalt-and-concrete

Simple but never stark, that's the message inherent in Gordon White's lovely garden. His driveway, which leads to a garage left of this photo, is a triumph of stone-fitting, resulting in a pattern that flows from the street and softens the clean, contemporary lines of the house. Plants are held to a minimum, not because Gordon isn't a serious gardener but because he intended them to enhance the space, not announce "I'm a garden."

The Southern Minimalist

Austin, Texas

run, was used for turning vehicles and moving them off the property. It was narrow for a residence driveway and the first owners – who used it for their car, Gordon slyly adds – intended to widen it some day. Gordon intended to widen it, too, and eliminate some of the obstructions, such as the copious amounts of granite gravel on the lot. He started by taking out the cinder blocks, turned sideways and deeply embedded in the ground, which edged the driveway. "Liriope grew out of the holes of the blocks, very pretty but not very functional because the sprinkler system didn't reach the plants," Gordon says. "So I took the blocks out and planted the liriope in drifts in the beds." That was only the beginning.

Gordon had become smitten with the original limestone steps leading to the gated entrance of the house. "They're exquisite," he says. "I wanted to somehow connect the driveway and the street to these beautiful steps, to follow through with some kind of flow and design."

He asked the former owners who had installed the steps, but they remembered him only as Talbot, who had given up stone masonry to build play spaces for children. Gordon took the common-sense route and looked in the Yellow Pages, under play spaces. One was listed as "Neverland," and he dialed the number. "Hey, it's Talbot," said the answering machine. "I'm not here right now...."

The inspiration for the stonework in Gordon White's garden was the step at the front door, installed by a stonemason when the house was built. Gordon has kept plant varieties to a minimum and repeats them throughout the garden. In the foreground: creeping pyracantha. Near the crape myrtle tree he grows holly fern, liriope, iris and purple-leafed oxalis, among other plants.

"Talbot – whose first name is James – put those steps in ten years before, but he remembered exactly where the house was, and he promised if I'd help he'd do a driveway for me," Gordon says.

Thus it began. "It turned out to be a larger area of stone than I'd anticipated, and we went out to the quarry to collect it all," Gordon says. "But there were three of us – four at one point – and it took us only two months to complete. That was in 1995. It does exactly what I wanted it to do – you get the feeling as you walk up the driveway of a flow toward the house and the garage. And the shadows of the trees overhead, the pecans and the cedar elms, cast a pattern of shade over the stone that adds to the mosaic look."

The gravel between the driveway and the peripheral plant borders also flows – in fact, Gordon thinks of it as a stream bed. "The whole plan, the curving driveway and the gravel, mimics the curve of the ravine on the other side," he says. And the Eastern mood was quite deliberate. For relaxation Gordon rakes the gravel to represent waves, as Japanese gardeners often do, using one of several rakes with various tine widths made for him by a man who helps him garden on weekends. "Everyone thinks I'm some kind of crazy gardener, especially the kids in the neighborhood," he laughs. "They say 'Dr. White, are you raking your water *again*?'"

To maintain continuity, the overall design repeats certain elements, from plants in spiky and rounded forms to the hard elements and design shapes. For instance, the

A small island rock topped with a changing arrangement of stones sits in the ziggurat shape of the driveway. It's sparingly planted with lamb's ears (*Stachys byzantina*), silver thyme (*Thymus* x *citriodorus* 'Silver Queen') and daffodils (only the foliage shows because the blooms have died). In the rear bed: the graceful lilyturf (*Liriope*) and a single hosta, which doesn't do well in the heat of Gordon's garden. The pink-toned crushed gravel in the dry stream bed is raked to resemble the waves in a real stream.

ziggurat pattern of the edge of the driveway echoes the limestone edging of the planting beds. Circles, curves and angular forms are repeated and play against each other, as in the curve of the driveway and the rectangular shape of the raised bed it encloses. The raised bed, in turn, is softened by a small rounded alcove on the far side (not seen in these photos), which contains a little Indonesian urn. Holly ferns are a common denominator throughout the garden, as are liriope, lycoris and crape myrtles. "A kind of continuity prevails," he says. "That's important with plants. My garden is shady, with morning sun and patches the rest of the day, and I think of it as a monochromatic, textural garden. When you get the hues in harmony, textures come to the fore, and a mood is established."

Gordon does like small spots of color, however, such as a planting of cobalt-blue iris among the liriope. Or the yellow rain lily (*Zephyranthes*), which stands out in green foliage – he jokes that it's becoming so popular and over-hybridized that it will soon be known as the daylily of the new millennium. He's fond of the crape myrtles' beautiful bark and white flowers. "A lot of people chop them off to get more bloom, but I let them grow. "If you leave them alone they develop a natural bonsai look."

Gordon loves a good lawn, but because of the dry climate he focused on stone, crushed gravel and drought-tolerant plants. Yet he's the only resident on his street without an expanse of water-guzzling grass, despite frequent water restrictions. A couple of years ago he went on a garden tour to Santa Fe with the Garden Conservancy of America and was both surprised and disappointed to find all the gardens selected were on irrigation systems in the middle of a drought. "I guess it was obvious how I felt," he says. "Some of the people on the trip had to sit on me to get me to keep my mouth shut." ■

Most people seeing Lee and Ross Jamieson's garden for the first time comment on its Oriental look. "Well, I can't disagree with that, but we planned it as an Alberta landscape, like what we see outside Edmonton," Lee says. It also wasn't intended to be a minimalist or low-maintenance garden, although it's both of these even if the mature plants give the garden a fuller look than when it was planted eight years ago.

It took Lee and Ross a few years to decide exactly what they wanted to do with their front yard, although they knew it needed improvement. When they moved into the post-war bungalow the front yard had two pretty flowering crab apple trees and rock-hard soil supporting a struggling lawn. "It was okay when the trees were in bloom, but after that it seemed like the sidewalk and the street were right in my face," says Lee.

She tried cosmetic measures like a raised planter under the living room window and flower beds around the sidewalk, but nothing really softened the look of the bare grass. Then her friend Asbjorg Vandermeer, who has since gone on to become a professional garden designer, started drawing up plans. "The first one she numbered Jamieson Garden 0001, and it couldn't have been a truer prediction," laughs Lee. "It was very nice, but we weren't ready. This kept happening even after we decided to go ahead ... just as we'd be about to start, she'd say hold on, I have a new plan."

Early in the process, however, it became evident that the house was a big part of the problem. For one thing, the foundation showed. "In the rainy tropics they have an excuse for

The Year-Round Garden
Edmonton, Alberta

houses on stilts," complains Lee with a laugh. "But I don't understand why they have to be so high here in Canada – the foundations always look separated from the rest of the house." To tie the two together, she painted the house and the naked concrete foundation a restful blue-gray.

Then they addressed the straight and narrow concrete path and the tiny front door stoop, which barely held one person and was made more awkward because the door is tucked into the ell of the house and opens toward the side. Asbjorg suggested a more expansive treatment: a wider, slightly curved path in charcoal gray pavers to complement the house, and a large entrance deck in warm cedar, flanked with steps on both sides to allow access from either direction. "Our property slopes down to the street, which made the house look even higher than it is," says Lee. "Widening the steps and adding the deck made everything more horizontal and took away from the feeling that the house was on stilts."

The first plans included terracing and flower beds, but these evolved to the present emphasis on a landscape of cool greens and lots of texture in plants and rocks. Lee also wanted a garden that looked good in fall and winter, and that led them to shrubs and evergreens with interesting growth forms. "You limit yourself if you plant for spring and summer in this climate," she says. "Spring is almost non-existent and summers are only reasonable, but we have

Lee and Ross Jamieson's front yard wasn't designed to have an Oriental look or require minimal maintenance, although it has both qualities. What the couple really had in mind was a garden that reflected the landscape of Alberta. For continuity, Lee planted the boulevard with a dwarf blue spruce, hosta and iris, and the sidewalk was extended to carry the garden's theme to the street. The abundance of foliage and spare color scheme give the garden serenity.

lovely long falls and endless winters. As our plan developed, Asbjorg left me lots of options to put things in or not, as I wished. I began to feel that using too many flowers would be embellishing – just like when I'm dressing to go out, I always finish by taking off half the jewelry I've put on."

To skew the view slightly sideways and take away from the squared look of the plan, Asbjorg designed a dry stream bed that "flows" diagonally through the garden from the corner of the deck to the sidewalk. A cedar ramp was built over the stream bed near the deck to allow access through the garden to the back gate, without having to go up one side of the steps and down the other. "Most people call it a bridge," says Lee, "but to me it's a pier, like at an Alberta lake. Piers and creeks always have bulrushes and grassy plants growing around them, so I planted iris along the stream bed for the same idea."

The rock-hard soil was dug up and the landscape contoured and covered with landscape cloth to reduce weed growth. Asbjorg and Lee went to a local quarry to choose rock and Asbjorg supervised the installation. Pit run, a mixture of sand and gravel, was poured 6 to 8 inches deep over the whole space and tamped down firmly. Lee dug right through the landscape fabric to plant globe and 'Brandon' cedars, 'Goldflame' spirea, red- and yellow-twig dogwood, plus a variegated-leaf dogwood, tall 'Wichita Blue' and creeping 'Prince of Wales' juniper, bird's-nest spruce, mugo pine, purpleleaf sand cherry and more. She planted ribbon grass for its green and white stripe, but it's reverting to solid green and becoming invasive, so feather reed may take its place.

Hostas, thymes, coral bells, 'Dragon's Blood' sedum, ferns and astilbe also have a subtle presence in the garden, as well as lily of the valley. "Another invasive plant," says Lee. "But you can't beat the perfume."

She learned a lesson with the ground cover bearberry, or kinnikinick, which becomes a glorious red with leaves and berries in fall. It died back a little every year and just wasn't thriving, no matter how well they cared for the garden, raking away dead material in fall and making sure there were no sanctuaries for insects or small animals. Then they started ignoring the garden a little, leaving dropped leaves and twigs as winter mulch. "Suddenly the kinnikinick started to grow," says Lee. "The lesson is to go with nature." Now she and Ross clean out only the creek bed in fall, leaving the main clean-up till spring, after most bits have broken down.

The unexpected bonus of the front garden is its year-round attraction from the house, Lee says. "If all you have is grass in this climate, it'll be green for a while in spring, then you get brown for a long time in summer. Then it's white, for a *really* long time. If the sun shines on the snow it blinds you, and if it's dull it's really depressing.

"But in this garden there's something to look at all the time, from red dogwood twigs to mounding pines and rocks with character. In summer it's a much nicer ambiance than flat grass along the sidewalk to the street. From inside you feel surrounded by green. If I ever have another front garden, I'll design it from my living room." ▪

Interest is maintained in winter with a small conifer, grasses and seedheads. The new front stoop and two-directional steps and the presence of rocks are important elements in the summer as well as the winter garden.

Southwest Cool

Opposite: There's a simple but sophisticated look to this nature-friendly garden in Phoenix, Arizona. It follows the principles of xeriscaping, which emphasizes the use of water-thrifty plants adapted to the local environment and more mulch to retain the moisture in the ground, with no lawn. Both the plantings and the house evoke the desert at a glance. The elegant, pale terra-cotta stucco home, trimmed in warm wood, is set off perfectly by a native saguaro cactus (*Carnegiea gigantea*), which is a good example of how a single tree in a garden can have more impact than two. The verbena at the base of the cactus, also a native plant, picks up on the rosy tone of the stucco.

Flower Power

Above: Minimalist gardens are not necessarily austere. Many, including this garden in Encinitas, California, employ an array of colorful flowers. The secret in maintaining the minimalist look is disciplined planting and pruning that shows off each species, plus a mulch such as fine gravel that separates each plant. This garden also has a special feature that accommodates the dry, Mediterranean climate: during a rainy spell, a gravel-lined pond under the raised ramp to the front door captures the rainwater from the roof, then diverts it into a stream bed that flows through the front garden and drains through the gravel to the earth below. In dry spells, the pond and stream take on the personality of their counterparts in the desert. The owner, a serious gardener, has chosen lavender, delosperma (a daisy-flowered succulent), diascia and lamb's ears (*Stachys byzantina* 'Helene von Stein', foreground) as bedding plants. A dwarf navel orange grows in the pot beside the entrance ramp.

Creating a Minimalist Garden

"A garden is a thing of beauty and a job forever," goes an old saying. Well, there's less danger of the latter in a minimalist garden, with lots of gravel used as flooring, a few rocks and carefully placed, low-maintenance plants. Still, be warned that there's no such thing as a no-maintenance garden – or plant, for that matter.

Minimalist Garden Guidelines

- Look to the Japanese for inspiration. Many minimalist gardens unconsciously borrow from the finely honed Oriental esthetic.
- Pretend you're packing for a vacation and do what the experts do: cut back your list of garden plants by half.
- If you prefer something green to gravel as your garden's essential floor covering, plant a ground cover that stays evergreen in your area or maintains some winter texture, such as thymes, vinca or ivy. Or consider shredded bark mulches, thickly laid. They aren't as stable as other materials or plants and they'll break down in a few years, but they suit some locations better than gravel and they have the advantage of being organic.
- One beautifully shaped tree is preferable to two because it becomes a focal point, especially if it's underscored with a few low, textured shrubs, a large rock or two and a beautiful urn.
- The exception: a double row of pleached trees – small-leaved varieties like linden limbed up to look like a hedge on stilts – that create an *allée* toward your front door, or frame a bench or statue.
- Use easy-care materials. Concrete can be given many faces. Mix it with gravel to create an aggregate, texture it with a wire brush while it's still wet or embed it with pebbles to make a mosaic, color it to resemble sandstone, or imprint it with large, coarsely veined leaves.
- Copper tubing makes interesting, simple arbors. Steel wire and aluminum rods can be used for pergolas.

One good chair makes an excellent focal point in a minimalist planting, especially when it's backed by a stunning, colorful plant, like these fluffy pink peonies (*Paeonia*). Hens and chicks (*Sempervivum tectorum*) creep between the flagstones and golden creeping Jenny (*Lysimachia nummularia* 'Aurea') spills over the front edge of the border.

Rock

Rock is an important element in the making of a minimalist garden. It has a strong, simple presence and can make a more emphatic statement than a whole bed of blowsy plants. But most people have trouble placing specimen rocks in the garden, leaving them to look like they just dropped off the truck. Too often they're placed as sentinels by the driveway, where they can look awkward or foreboding.

People who work with stone will tell you that each one has its face – that is, the side best presented to the viewer. It's hard for an amateur to recognize this, but the best advice is to look at your rock carefully, go for coffee and come back with a fresh eye. Ideally, you should do this before you have the rock delivered so you have some idea of how you'll place it in the garden. It helps if you can determine the rock's center of gravity and then imagine higher ground lines along the face of the rock to see how it will look buried in the soil.

This brings me to a big don't: Don't ever leave a rock, even a small one, perched on top of the soil. It will look unstable. You never see rocks this way in nature, unless they're about to fall or have just fallen down the side of a mountain. Embed them in the soil to about two-thirds their depth.

If you can, use the rule of odd numbers: place three, five or seven stones in a group. In Japanese design, groups of seven are sometimes broken into subgroups of three, two and two in the same area. The *sanzon* is a traditional Japanese arrangement using three stones – one tall one flanked by two smaller ones for balance – and often represents a waterfall.

Look for different shapes: tall verticals and low verticals; horizontal stones; and arching shapes, higher on one side than the other. Use them together in groups. Avoid white or pale gray stones – they stand out too strongly. An aged look is preferable for any garden. Don't place a rugged mountain stone next to a smooth, river-washed one.

Above all, look to nature for advice in placing stones. She is the best teacher.

Gravel

Gravel is an attractive and relatively inexpensive ground cover for a minimalist garden, as well as an effective mulch that holds in moisture and helps to smother weeds. It also fits the minimalist look, and different gravels present their own personalities.

Sharp-edged gravels are often the cheapest, but are hard to walk on, especially the bigger sizes. Rounded pea gravels are more friendly, especially the smaller-gauged choices.

Look for gravel that matches as much as possible the color of the larger rocks in your garden, or the brick of your house or pathways if you're not using rocks. Most gravel and rock sold in an area are indigenous, so this may not be a problem. Crushed red tile is lovely, but don't combine it with gray limestone specimen rocks. Their moods clash (to say nothing of their contrasting colors) because they come from different times and places.

Plants with presence and a variety of shapes and textures work well in minimalist gardens. Here, a selection of ferns, including maidenhair fern (*Adiantum pedatum*) in the foreground, softens the bristly contours of hens and chicks (*Sempervivum tectorum*) and a long-needled pine.

The Northern Messenger

For thousands of years the inukshuk has been used in Arctic regions to help herd caribou, point the way to travelers or warn of dangerous places. Now they're becoming popular – and easily constructed – focal points in southern gardens, like the one in the Edmonton garden above.

The optimum height is three or four feet, and the form generally has a human look, especially if there is a main stone jutting out near the shoulder area, like an arm pointing out a specific direction.

Like all forms of sculpture or garden art, inukshuks are individually made, but here are a few guidelines:

- To avoid lugging home tons of stone and then finding you don't have the right pieces, try to roughly construct the piece where you obtain the stone. Then photograph it, disassemble it and reconstruct it on site.
- Use any kind of stone that blends with your garden, which probably means the local variety. Be sure the pieces have two flat sides so they'll stack.
- Put the heaviest rocks on the bottom for a sturdy base, and for stability embed them to two-thirds of their depth.
- Follow the human form, starting with legs, a pelvis of one big stone topped by two verticals (as above) and a stack of smaller stones to represent the torso. You may want a wider stone for shoulders or arms, topped with smaller specimens for a head. But be creative: even three stones – a strong vertical for the lower body topped with a horizontal stone and a smaller round one to represent the head – makes a simple, workable inukshuk.
- Feel free to change the composition if the mood strikes or the set-up doesn't look quite right.

Plants

A minimalist garden has a sophisticated air. Focus on strong, simply shaped evergreens and avoid fancy topiary shapes, like spirals and pompoms. However, prune both evergreens and deciduous trees or shrubs with an eye for bringing out the lines of the trunk or branches. Keep flowering perennials on the subdued side: no garish colors or floppy, overgrown growth habits. For low maintenance choose plants indigenous to your area.

Foamflower

Hens and chicks

Evergreens

bird's-nest spruce (*Picea abies* 'Nidiformis')
camellia (*Camellia japonica*)
holly (*Ilex*)
mugo pine (*Pinus mugo*)
rhododendrons and azaleas (*Rhododrendron*)
tall pines (*Pinus nigra, P. aristata, P. strobus*)

Small Trees

cherry (*Prunus*)
corkscrew hazel (*Corylus avellana* 'Contorta')
crab apple (*Malus*)
Eastern redbud (*Cercis canadensis*)
euonymus (*Euonymus alatus*)
Japanese maple (*Acer palmatum*)
mountain ash (*Sorbus americana*)
paperbark maple (*Acer griseum*)
Siberian peashrub standard (*Caragana arborescens*)
white birch (*Betula pendula*)

Soft Shapes

artemisia (*Artemisia*)
foamflower (*Tiarella cordifolia*)
golden variegated hakonechloa grass (*Hakonechloa macra* 'Aureola')
Japanese blood grass (*Imperata cylindrica* 'Red Baron')
Japanese painted fern (*Athyrium niponicum* 'Pictum')
maidenhair fern (*Adiantum pedatum*)
meadow rue (*Thalictrum*)
mosquito grass (*Bouteloua gracilis*)
rock rose (*Helianthemum*)
small leaved hostas (*Hosta sieboldii* 'Ginko Craig', *H.* 'Ground Sulphur')
thread-leaved coreopsis (*Coreopsis verticillata*)

Spikes

Adam's needle (*Yucca filamentosa*)
blazing star (*Liatris spicata*)
daylilies (*Hemerocallis*)
grasses (*Calamagrostis* x *acutiflora* 'Karl Foerster', *Festuca glauca* and *Schizachyrium scoparium*)
iris (*Iris germanica, I. sibirica, I. ensata*)
lilyturf (*Liriope*)
'The Rocket' ligularia (*Ligularia stenocephala* 'The Rocket')
sedge (*Carex buchananii*)
Spanish bayonet (*Yucca glauca*)

Plants with Presence

bear's breeches (*Acanthus mollis*)
bergenia (*Bergenia cordifolia*)
giant hosta (*Hosta* 'Sum and Substance,' *H. montana macrophylla*)
large masterwort (*Astrantia maxima*)
ornamental rhubarb (*Rheum palmatum* var. *tanguticum*)
sea hollies (*Eryngium giganteum, E. planum*)
sea kale (*Crambe cordifolia*)
yucca (see Spikes, above)

Chapter Nine

Fusion Gardens

There's something to be said for a nice patch of grass, despite the fact that large lawns are the antithesis of this book. A properly placed circle or oval of grass can

pull a garden together just as an area rug unifies the arrangement of furniture in a living room. The great gardens of seventeenth-century France were good examples of this principle, with their *tapis verts* (little green carpets of grass) dividing yet holding together stylized rose gardens, formal ponds and potagers (stylized vegetable gardens).

Most people don't look at grass this way. They consider it the filler between the flower beds and don't give its shape much thought at all. It ends up as the predictable square in the middle of the yard, with plant borders all around. Sometimes the garden itself is in transition as it gradually metamorphoses from a conventional foundation planting to a full-fledged front garden, so the gardener deliberately ignores the poor grass, allowing its esthetics to disappear in the process. The gardeners in this chapter, however, have taken the Le Nôtre approach and designed the grass to complement the garden, fusing the elements together into one eye-pleasing design. The grass is an integral part of the whole.

It could be said that all good gardens demand fusion of one kind or another. The elements of color, shape, form and texture in plants and harder elements blend to create a design on a larger scale that is more than the sum of its parts. In this chapter I focus on gardeners who have mastered different kinds of fusion particularly well. It all goes to prove that in a garden, as in life, confidence and creativity count as much as rules, which are sometimes made to be broken.

In fusion gardens grass works as an anchor or a restful change of pace. Opposite: Beds are separated by grass paths and contain a succession of plants: in spring, red and yellow tulips, Virginia bluebells (*Mertensia virginica*) and white-blooming sweet woodruff (*Galium odoratum*). Above: The grass is an oval carpet centering a bed of *Anemone sylvestris* and dwarf Korean lilac (*Syringa meyeri* 'Palibin').

JAN AND JOHN TRIMBLE admit they're zealous gardeners, but there was a time they felt dominated by their thirsty, ravenous expanse of lawn. That was in their former home, where they had a fairly conventional landscape typical of their neighborhood: a large swath of grass set off by sweeping beds of azaleas edged with clumps of impatiens.

"We loved that garden for many reasons," says Jan. "It was pretty as a postcard. But eventually we got to thinking that it was as dead as a postcard, too."

With a landscape-style garden, the goal is to bring the design and plantings to perfection and freeze it there. Unlike less formal, flowery gardens, which change with the gardener's whim and the weather, the Trimbles' large lawn and shrub borders remained static. "And we're gardeners, we yearned for a change," says Jan.

In 1992, the opportunity for change arose when the Trimbles began building a new home. They decided to go natural to reflect the native limestone of the area and the rocky, scrub-covered lot, and while the carpenters were still hammering they impulsively sold all their lawn equipment. "We picked up two splendid books – Sally and Andy Wasowski's *Native Texas Plants* and Scott Ogden's *Gardening Success with Difficult Soils*, and started studying native plants and the world of xeriscape," Jan says.

It soon became apparent, however, that old habits die

The Trimbles' subtle yet colorful garden co-operates with nature: the square carpets of buffalo grass (*Buchloe dactyloides*) in these pictures needed little feeding and less mowing, but it's been replaced with Asian jasmine (*Trachelospermum asiaticum*), a ground cover that's proved to be even tougher. The other plants in the garden last through heat and drought like troopers. Beds are mounded with lantana (*Lantana montevidensis*), a dependable bloomer; 'White Star' zinnia; two varieties of muhly grass (*Muhlenbergia capillaris* and *M. lindheimeri*); 'Blue Victory' annual salvia in center of photo; and tall *Salvia leucantha*, near trees in background.

An English Garden, Texas Style

Austin, Texas

hard. Just a little lawn, please, each was thinking, and something not quite so loose – we want a little more structure in the garden, too. "In our unregenerate hearts we were still pining for a verdant garden, something green and lush and with eye-filling color," Jan says almost apologetically. "To be honest, what we wanted was an English cottage garden."

And because they'd felt overwhelmed with the care of their previous garden, lower water bills and lower maintenance were also priorities. The trick, as they learned, was to co-operate with Mother Nature by choosing the right plants for their conditions.

They re-evaluated their approach to design and added visual interest and structure to the new garden with paths. "They're not wide ones, only about 18 inches, but they act as room dividers for access to the plants and definition in the garden," says Jan. "In summer they almost disappear as the plants spill over them, but they really show up in winter, when the perennials are cut back. The stone paths, the big rocks we've used, the grasses and the beautiful dark hardwood mulch we put down make a beautiful picture in winter and show up the architecture of the garden."

The slightly curved main path from the street to an inviting front porch moves through glorious beds jam-packed with grasses (Gulf muhly, liriope, Indian grass, 'Hameln' dwarf fountain grass) and huge mounds of lantana, and passes by large carpets of buffalo grass. "It goes

three weeks without mowing, and needs feeding only a couple of times a year," says Jan. "But it's proved to be not as thick or resilient as our former St. Augustine grass. Still, it's plenty lovely when it ripples in the breeze." (The buffalo grass also proved to allow weeds in, and since these photos were taken has been replaced with Asian jasmine, a dark green creeping ground cover that's hardy as nails, Jan says, and takes foot traffic.)

Near the house more wide beds take over and an incredible Queen's wreath coral vine nearly covers the garage and the porch. "It's really a fast grower in warm weather," says Jan. "It dies back a bit in fall so I cut it to the ground for winter, and it can grow 10 feet in three weeks once spring comes. I have to wire it up to hold it."

Jan and John put in months of back-breaking labor the first year, designing and installing their garden themselves, because that's what they like to do. After a couple of years of on-site editing, they had a garden that pleased them, with plants that combined both beauty and toughness. "Some of them, like the lantana, hymenoxys and artemisia, I swear could survive in a furnace," says Jan. "When it's 100 degrees in summer and hasn't rained in three weeks, the lantana is still blooming like crazy."

In fact, gardening these days consists of deadheading, pruning and sitting on the porch or back deck to enjoy their handiwork, a drought-resistant, hardier version of an English cottage garden. All in all, it's a welcome state of affairs. ■

Opposite: Grasses such as gulf muhly, Lindheimer muhly (*Muhlenbergia capillaris* and *M. lindheimeri*) and feather grass (*Stipa tenuissima*) dominate the beds, which are divided by paths and covered with hardwood mulch to retain moisture. *Salvia leucantha* branches over the bed top right. Right: Coral vine (*Antigonon leptopus*) ramps over the porch roof; 'White Star' zinnia and Madagascar periwinkle (*Catharanthus roseus*) bloom below.

Tips from the Trimbles
- Use vines freely and let them intermarry.
- Use berms, or small hills of earth, to offer topographical variety in a flat garden and to increase soil depth in a rocky garden.
- Repeat plantings of ornamental grasses throughout your garden. They supply informal accents and add lovely movement in a breeze.
- Use big rocks as accents, too. They require no water or fertilizer and give the eye plenty to enjoy in winter. For a special effect in a large bed, plant in groups of three, Japanese style.

- Let stuff run into other stuff. Cottage gardens are meant to be a profuse jumble of color and form. The sense of order should be provided by structural elements such as paths that contain the plantings, and repeated drifts or informal masses of shrubs.

LOVE BLOOMED in Rose Stepanko's former garden a decade or so ago, when Barry Lastiwka came to call. He'd come at Rose's request, as a landscape contractor and owner of a garden center, to help beautify her small plot. The plot thickened, as they say, and soon Rose and Barry were looking for their own place.

Naturally, it had to offer good potential for the two avid gardeners; additional priorities were an established neighborhood with mature trees. "We were smitten with this place the first moment we saw it," says Rose, "even though it looked like a campsite." The eighty-year-old brick house was set back on a nearly untouched lot on a street lined with American elms, and was shaded by several old trees: a graceful mountain ash that reached halfway across the front, a 40-foot cedar at the side of the house and a huge willow that spread its limbs over the small rear yard. That's the trouble with trees – sometimes they offer too much shade for serious gardeners.

But Barry and Rose soon developed a plan: the back would be fenced in and given over almost completely to a small private area for cooking and entertaining, and the front would be where they lived out most of their gardening fantasies. Under the mountain ash they'd make a spring garden, where flowers could bloom their pretty heads off till the tree leafed out; in summer, interest would shift to the sunny south side of the front yard, just inside a tall, protective caragana hedge, where they would plant their favorite perennials.

Placing plants in conditions they like, where they'll grow best, is a matter of common sense, but sometimes it takes the expertise of a horticulturist like Barry to actually plan things this way from the beginning. "Barry also knew

Love in a Cold Climate

Edmonton, Alberta

we had to start with basics like the architecture of the garden," says Rose. "Originally there was a straight concrete sidewalk leading to the house and it wasn't very inviting. So Barry designed a wider one of interlocking brick that winds a little and encourages you to stroll slowly to the front steps. There it divides and the arms go around to the back of the house on each side." The paths pass under classically designed arbors with ingenious inner workings – thought up by Barry, of course: each hides an eavestrough that carries water away from the house to drain into downspouts and weeping tiles at the lot lines. "This is an old house and we have to be careful of allowing dampness to get into the brick or the foundation," Rose says. The arbors, now covered by nearly ten years of vine growth, have the effect of visually extending the width of the house.

Barry also built short entrance pillars with lanterns, using leftover house bricks they found on the property, and enclosed and defined the front garden with an iron fence. "Then we planted about forty shrubs to create background and soften the house foundations," Rose says. "Near the mountain ash we put in several red-twig dogwood to contrast with the tree's winter berries – the twigs seem to get more red as the snow is melting and look even more lovely than in the dead of winter. We also put in hydrangea and dwarf Korean lilac, which are underplanted with purple

Rose Stepanko and Barry Lastiwka love their grass for its cool feeling on bare feet and its pleasant contrast to the flower beds, filled in spring with *Anemone sylvestris*. An oval patch of lawn is part of the garden's overall design, bisected by a curving path to the front door.

In spring, the garden bench offers a fragrant sitting spot perfumed with dwarf Korean lilacs (*Syringa meyeri* 'Palibin'), above. The charming old house is framed with a beautifully pruned mountain ash (*Sorbus americana*) and a white-painted iron fence, below.

tulips. In the spring the scent and color are overwhelming, all purple and mauve, with the big drifts of white *Anemone sylvestris* under the mountain ash."

The anemone dominates the spring garden, one of the two large flower beds whose shapes were established by the negative edge of the oval central lawn. "We couldn't give up having some grass, much as we like to garden," Rose says. "It feels so cool on bare feet, and contrasts with the rest of the garden, especially when everything else is dormant. But Barry would never have a square of grass in the middle – he likes curving lines, they're more friendly and natural than geometric shapes. So our grass has an egg shape, placed on a bit of a slant and bisected by the path. There's an asymmetric look to it."

The plants were as carefully planned as the shape of the beds. Barry and Rose wanted low-growing spring plants in front of the fence and put in creeping baby's breath, blue-toned veronica, grape hyacinths and a mauve variety of *Clematis alpina* around the pillars. These plantings blend into the large beds, but it's the huge planting of soft white anemone that stops passersby in spring. "We tried so many different things, but the anemone worked best in the shade. It naturalizes beautifully, and if it gets out of hand all I do to control it is pull some out. It has fluffy seedheads in fall, so it gives us a two-season look, and it's pest free and demands no maintenance."

The anemone is a good example of the couple's approach to planting – they plant in large groups of one variety instead of single plants dotted here and there. This is especially important in a small garden, where sweeps of one variety can capitalize on the effect of a subtle plant. In the sunny summer border to the right of the pathway Rose sticks to a yellow, white and blue color scheme, with big clumps of tall blue and white delphiniums, yellow coreopsis, white lilies and blue catmint. "The catmint is a real find for people who love lavender but can't grow it in our climate," she says. "Lavender always looks so small and pitiful here, if it manages to survive, and the catmint is a good lookalike."

Garden Plan

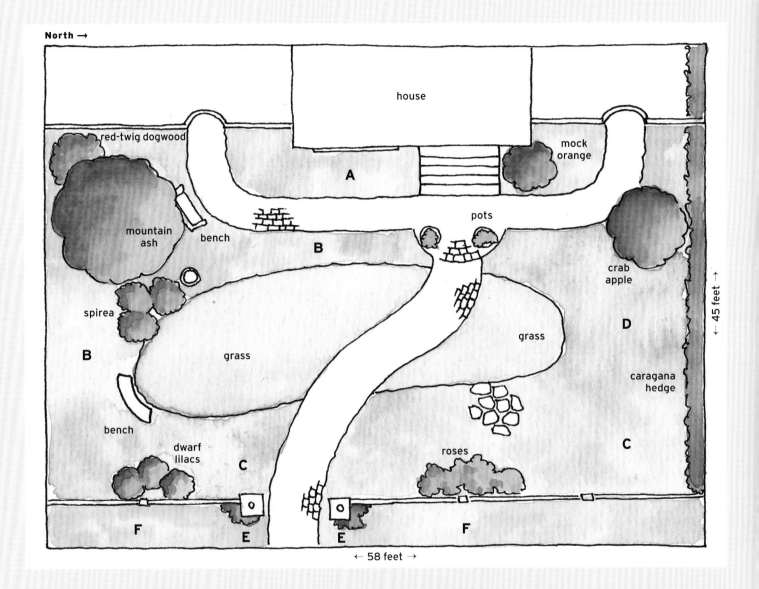

A 'The Rocket' ligularia and honeysuckle

B white anemone and blue forget-me-not

C creeping baby's breath, snow-in-summer and thyme

D yarrow, delphinium, catmint, heliopsis, Asiatic and Oriental lilies

E clematis growing over lampposts

F dianthus, candytuft, moss phlox

The border also contains some airy see-through plants, such as baby's breath, vining plants like clematis, which she experiments with to see what will survive, and a few roses for accents of pink. She's had the most success with the Canadian-bred 'Winnipeg Parks', a hardy deep rose variety in the Parkland series of shrub roses. The soil is banked upward from the pathway both for the best viewing effect and to optimize the sun, and ground-hugging woolly thyme and snow-in-summer, a sometimes invasive plant, soften the lines of the bed near the entrance.

"It's funny, I always refer to this as the July border, as if that's the only time it looks good," Rose says. "But there's something about it in the spring ... it has a few tulips, but it also has all those lovely mounds of green perennials starting to emerge. It has textural interest, but mainly it has promise." ∎

Opposite: Ligularia (*Ligularia stenocephala* 'The Rocket') shows off in the foundation bed in mid-summer, beckoning a gardener to sit a while on the Hansel-and-Gretel bench beside the path to the back garden. Above: A view of the same bench from inside the back garden. Barry designed the arbors, which hide extensions of the eavestrough; they carry water to downspouts at the lot line. Below: Catmint (*Nepeta faassenii* 'Six Hills Giant') doubles as lavender in Rose's July border.

Paths of Glory

Sometimes the beds in a lawn keep expanding till they take over the lot, which is what happened in this Toronto garden. Essentially it's a traditional front yard with flower beds lining the front walk, a foundation planting and perimeter beds adjoining a hedge along the lot line, all separated by lawn. But in this garden the beds have grown over the years so they have become more important than the grass. What's especially appealing is the care that's been taken to plan all-season bloom. In spring, above and left, many-colored tulips, Virginia bluebell (*Mertensia virginica*), sweet woodruff (*Galium odoratum*), forget-me-not (*Myosotis*), dainty pale-pink perennial geranium and bolder rose-pink allium bring cheer. In summer, opposite, the large leaves of hostas and spiky blue penstemon (*Penstemon digitalis*) have a more subtle style.

Plant Fusion

Opposite: Just a couple of plant varieties can be used to make a patterned and unusual front garden. A creative gardener in Thunder Bay, Ontario, combines wide bands of Virginia creeper (*Parthenocissus quinquefolia*) and low-growing juniper (*Juniperus horizontalis*) to make a two-toned green garden with a dramatic, swirling pattern. In fall, the Virginia creeper turns flaming red before it loses its leaves to reveal dark purple berries. The juniper maintains its cool tone all year round.

Above: An Ottawa, Ontario, house shows a happy face to the street with unusual red-and-blue painted trim complemented by a blend of mat-forming thymes: the rosy *Thymus praecox* 'Coccineus', grayish woolly thyme (*Thymus praecox* 'Pseudolanuginosus') and of a white-blooming variety *Thymus serpyllum*. The thymes keep their leaf texture and a muted color in winter, when the evergreens take over the visual effect.

Plants: Grass Alternatives

Typical lawn grasses aren't the first choice of many gardeners who want the rich, cool look of green in their gardens. Grass needs cutting and feeding, it goes dormant in mid-summer in many climates and it often doesn't do well in shady conditions. On top of that, it takes on a flat, dull look in cold-climate winter gardens and will suffer if walked upon in soggy springs.

A healthy stand of thick grass has one advantage over other ground covers, however: it bounces back from the wear and tear of children's summer play, and even a small patch is all you need for a game of catch or a round of wrestling. Still, many ground covers offer a more textured leaf and an evergreen presence, and few need any maintenance. For a front yard garden where children don't play, here are some decorative and sturdy green alternatives.

▼ **Baltic ivy** (*Hedera helix* 'Baltica')
Excellent in shade, many ivies maintain a dark, bronzy green color in winter and form a dense ground cover in moderate climates. In warm climates it can grow almost rapaciously. Also used as a vine.

▲ **Bearberry or kinnikinick**
(*Arctostaphylos uva-ursi*)
Especially popular in the Canadian prairies, bearberry produces a low carpet of shiny dark green leaves and sprays of fragrant pink flowers followed by red berries. It likes sun but tolerates shade, and although it takes a while to establish, one plant can cover a 5-foot circle.

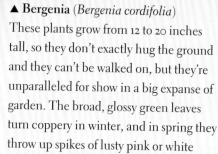

▲ **Bergenia** (*Bergenia cordifolia*)
These plants grow from 12 to 20 inches tall, so they don't exactly hug the ground and they can't be walked on, but they're unparalleled for show in a big expanse of garden. The broad, glossy green leaves turn coppery in winter, and in spring they throw up spikes of lusty pink or white blooms. They like sun or shade.

Bugleweed (*Ajuga reptans*)
In the garden it can be invasive, but as a patch of ground cover it fills an area quickly with above-ground runners. The rosettes of bronzy or deep green leaves, about 4 inches high, throw up fat spikes of pretty deep-blue flowers in early summer, and remain in winter, although the color darkens. Takes partial shade, and likes any soil.

False strawberry (*Duchesnea indica*)
Similar to wild strawberry, but with smaller leaves and inedible fruit. It spreads by runners and can be invasive. Small, yellow flowers. Will withstand some foot traffic; semi-evergreen in most climates.

▼ **Japanese spurge** (*Pachysandra terminalis*)
A classic, generally evergreen ground cover with fans of leaves growing 8 to 10 inches tall. Hardy, tolerant of drought, and the plants fill in with underground runners, although it may take a while to do so. Small white flowers in spring are very tiny, but add to the plant's overall appeal.

▶ **Periwinkle** (*Vinca minor*)
A prostrate ground cover with small, glossy evergreen leaves and lilac-blue flowers in spring. It takes a couple of years to establish itself but does well in both sun and partial shade, and likes moist sandy loam. Not hardy in severe winters.

▲ **Sweet woodruff** (*Galium odoratum*)
A sweet little low-growing plant with whorls of light green leaves and snowy white flowers in spring. In medieval times it was used to flavor wine. The plant takes a while to establish but loves shade and slightly acid soil, and gives an airy look to any garden. Plants are visible in winter and send up fresh green shoots in spring.

Thyme (*Thymus*)
Except for the culinary thyme you'll want to grow in a pot beside the kitchen door, most thymes grow low enough to create a mat of plants in a garden and maintain a muted color and texture in winter.

A mosaic of varieties is especially appealing – woolly thyme (*Thymus praecox* 'Pseudolanuginosus'), lemon thyme (*T. x citriodorus*), and *T. praecox* 'Coccineus'. Your nursery will have many varieties to choose from.

White clover (*Trifolium repens*)
Lawn purists consider this a weed, but when the grass goes brown it's what provides green foliage in most lawns. A low, creeping durable perennial with three-part leaves and sweetly scented white flowers that attract bees, it also is a nitrogen fixer that improves soil. Why don't we love it?

Chapter Ten

Natural Gardens

Every garden is a natural garden because it's a product of nature, but in today's need to identify trends the name has taken on a broader meaning. Or meanings,

to be exact: at one end of the scale are those purists who believe that a natural garden should contain only native plants that grew in North America before Columbus discovered it in 1492. This severely narrows their choices while veering awfully close to plant xenophobia. At the other end are the lazy gardeners, who prefer to think natural means letting things go and allowing nature to have its way. In the process they raise their neighbors' ire and give the whole movement toward gardening in tune with nature a bad name.

I'm pretty much in the middle. In my terms, a natural garden is closely tied to the terrain, climate and native plant life of the site, but the hand of the gardener is inherent in the design. In short, it's environmentally friendly, common-sense gardening, using plants that thrive in your garden's conditions and planting them in a design that recreates nature as much as is practical in your neighborhood. At its best, a natural garden copies a scene from nature: a prairie or a meadow, a desert, a woodland, a rocky mountain scene. As in nature, plant form and texture, bark, fruits and seedheads all play an important role in the dynamics of the garden. And as we cultivate, deadhead and prune our natural gardens – for they need this kind of care as much as conventional gardens do – we learn valuable lessons about the mysterious and wondrous interactions between all living things, even in our own front yards.

Natural gardens can thrive in the city and please the neighbors as well as the gardener. Opposite: Yellow coneflowers (*Rudbeckia*) and blazing star (*Liatris*) are part of an urban prairie that attracts butterflies, birds, bees and dragonflies. Above: Ferns, foamflower (*Tiarella cordifolia*) and trillium (*Trillium grandiflorum*) in a shaded garden in spring.

A COUPLE OF YEARS before she was due to retire, Helen McKean did something that wouldn't enter the heads of most seniors: she sold the efficient condominium apartment she'd been living in and bought a ranch-style house – on a 100-by-150-foot lot. "I bought it because I didn't want a big lot," she says, somewhat surprised that anyone would think this was a big lot, and then wonder why she'd add to her workload when most people would be cutting back. "The condo was fine when I was working because I traveled a lot, but I'd always liked gardening and I decided I wanted a place where I had room to drag around a shovel. Gardening brings me peace, and that's what I wanted to do."

Helen says her lot might be considered large in Madison, but in Appleton, it's just average. And she had plans: she'd attended a few seminars on gardening with native plants and had made a commitment to herself to plant a prairie garden. "I just felt, given all I'd been hearing, that this kind of garden was better for the environment," she says. It meant growing indigenous plants in large, natural stands, as they might grow in nature; once established, they'd need no extra watering, no special feeding and no pesticides.

Some people think prairie gardens are messy gardens that contribute to a slummy-looking street, especially if they're in the front. "In Madison some people have even cut down their neighbors' prairie gardens in the middle of the night," Helen says. The seminar leaders offered lots of strategies for coping with suspicious neighbors (including explaining your garden goals, making sure you're frequently

A Prairie Native

Appleton, Wisconsin

seen weeding and deadheading your small patch of prairie, and planting near the house to show how much you love the plants), but Helen hasn't had any problems – even though her garden almost blankets her corner lot, back, side and front. "My two immediate neighbors don't really care a lot about gardening and anything I do seems fine with them," she says. In fact, she's a little disappointed that her garden, started nearly a decade ago, hasn't inspired similar ones in her immediate area, which remains a vast sweep of lawns dotted with houses.

To separate a prairie from the neighbor's garden, the seminar leaders also advised the use of fences for discipline and pathways for structure. Helen took this advice and put in a 6-foot fence across the back of her lot, stepping it down to 4 feet along the street side to satisfy local bylaws, and she framed the front garden with a wide mown path in the grass between the garden and the street. Later she added a split-rail fence on the corner. "I think bare corners are ugly," she says.

Once the prairie natives were established they grew bountifully: bee balm and purple coneflower ramble from the house to the side fence in a medley of pink and mauve. Purple ironweed, yellow-branched coneflower, stiff goldenrod, Joe-Pye weed and more flow from the corner across the front, with marsh marigolds thriving with the Joe-Pye weed in the dampness of the drainage ditch. White

After attending a few seminars on gardening with native plants, Helen McKean was converted. Her corner lot is filled with prairie plants, including brown-eyed Susan (*Rudbeckia triloba*), purple ironweed (*Vernonia*) and Joe-Pye weed (*Eupatorium maculatum*). The cup plant (*Silphium perfoliatum*) likes the location so much it's grown past the eaves of the house.

Helen took the advice of her seminar leaders and framed the front garden with a strip of mown grass that extends into the ditch, above. Swamp milkweed (*Asclepias incarnata*) thrives in the damp soil.

Opposite: a lovely combination of wild mauve bee balm (*Monarda fistulosa*) and purple coneflower (*Echinacea purpurea*) fills the side garden from the fence to the house.

spires of Culver's root and accents of white false indigo show up throughout, balancing and separating the colors.

When Helen took possession of the lot it boasted a stand of six or more silver maples. "Awful trees," she says. "I'd never plant them." So she took them out, and met with only one eyebrow raised by a neighbor. "The man across the street looked a little worried," she says with a giggle. "I'm sure he wondered what was coming next."

What was coming were a few sumac shrubs planted with prairie dropseed on the advice of a consultant. It was a mistake. Almost immediately the sumac annihilated the grass and threatened to conquer the rest of the garden. Since then Helen has learned to do things on her own, and that includes introducing a few non-natives to her prairie gems: for example, a bed of much-loved roses and a few hybridized cultivars of bee balm. "Yes, I'm guilty," she says, clearly feeling free to do as she wants. "The roses went in a long time ago, and I added red and deep pink bee balm because I wanted more than just the native mauve. Besides, the cultivars are more resistant to mildew."

Opposite: In a group, the right choice of native flowering plants offers a colorful show, as in the combination of white Culver's root (*Veronicastrum virginicum*) and red bee balm (*Monarda didyma*) backed by wild mauve bee balm (*Monarda fistulosa*) and black-eyed Susan (*Rudbeckia hirta*). But single specimens have presence too, such as the mauve bee balm above, and golden ragwort (*Senecia aureus*) below.

The grass for the first bed, a strip about 25-by-60 feet at the back of the lot, was dispatched with a glyphosate herbicide, and then the soil was rototilled. "But only once, not twice over two years like they recommend. Actually, I did that whole bed the first year, even the seeding, because I was so impatient."

She kept the bed moist until germination started, then sat back and watched the seedlings grow. "I guess I was lucky and we had enough rain to keep things going, because I didn't water at all," she says. "You have to wait two or three years to see flowers from seed, so for the side and corner bed I ordered a collection of started plants, about 180 all told." This time she dispensed with the herbicide and laid down pads of newspaper covered with a thick layer of mulch to smother the grass. "It didn't work that well," she says. "The grass kept reappearing."

Live and learn. One thing Helen has learned is that she has soil that prairie plants thrive on. "Except for the purple prairie clover, which just disappeared after I planted it, everything really grows," she says. "The cup plant near the house is higher than the eaves, and the Culver's root, the goldenrod and purple coneflower keep moving around all over the place. And that brown-eyed Susan, which they used to call branched coneflower! It'll try to take over till I die."

She's also realized how tough prairie plants can be: in late summer droughts the grass on the front slope fades to beige and sometimes turns up its roots and expires. But not the prairie plants. "That's the wonderful thing about them," she says. "No matter how dry it gets, none of them die."

But Helen's greatest pleasure in her prairie is not the flowers or watching their pattern shift and change with nature, it's the wildlife it brings into her life, including a pair of now-resident warblers not usually seen in her region. "Even though this is a small garden in the middle of a whole bunch of lawns, the birds and butterflies somehow find it," she says. "I can imagine them flying over and looking down and saying to each other, 'That looks like an interesting place, let's just stop there a while.'" ■

Susan Como's front yard is more than just a garden. It's an experience – a mini-landscape meant to evoke the wondrous scenes Susan and her husband, Casey, trek through on their wilderness hikes in the front range of the Rocky Mountains near Edmonton. For Susan, an artist who works with fibers to create pieces that reflect the environment, it's also a living sculpture and a strong expression of her work.

For the birds, rabbits and other wildlife who drop by the garden it's both a sanctuary and a source of food. One day a lone deer wandered through (the couple live a block away from the North Saskatchewan River valley). "That was a lovely sight," Susan says. "Of course there was a downside – he ate all the daylily buds."

Visitors find the garden something of an adventure, which is the way Susan intended it. She contoured the earth with hills and valleys, designed a creek bed banked with rocks, planted stands of trees and shrubs as they'd be seen in nature, placed driftwood as it might have fallen naturally, and grouped flowers to weave together in a subtle mosaic. "I didn't want people to notice everything right at the start," she says. "First, they enter the garden from the street through shrubs 5 or 6 feet high. Then they discover the rest, moving downward into the center of the garden, a low area with the creek bed, rocks and sand, grasses and thymes. Next is the circular patio and then the land moves upward, with trees and shrubs and flowers. I wanted the sense of a vista, where people would view a sweep of land, something for the eye to move slowly through, and then rest on little areas of discovery." The vista is just as pleasing to the eye from the living room windows as from inside the garden, which was also intended.

From the street, Susan Como's garden invites you in to explore the landscape. It's been contoured with mini-hills and valleys and a dry creek bed, with driftwood placed as it might have fallen, to replicate nature.

A Natural Landscape
Edmonton, Alberta

When the Comos moved into the ranch-style bungalow in 1997 they inherited the usual flat lawn, large specimen tree and a couple of shrubs. "There was nothing to look at," says Susan. "My philosophy is: if you don't have a view, create one." So she began planning right away.

Her immediate task was to take out the tree and shrubs, only saving a lovely old mountain ash that still produces bright red winter berries. The established neighborhood had lots of existing trees that provided a sense of permanence, including a stand of spruce on the lot to the south. To the north the exposure was sunny. "I wanted both sun and shade plants, so this was good," Susan says.

The first year they devoted their energies to clearing the lot and removing the old soil to a depth of two feet, down to hard clay. New topsoil was brought in, and to it was added sand, compost and manure. "If you start off with good soil, you reap the benefits later," says Susan. She'd decided on a lowered creek bed, lower than the sidewalk running past their house, with raised banks. "This is how it would be in nature," she says, "or it wouldn't be a creek." The new soil was contoured to accommodate the different elevations.

"The first year we created the setting, the lay of the land, including putting in the hard elements like the round patio near the house," says Susan. For the patio they chose manufactured pavers that blend with the adjacent sand and

the soft red and ocher mix of bricks on the house. The smaller rocks were collected on hikes, from Susan's father's property and from farmers' fields. The bigger ones were obtained, with permission, from a mountain road-blasting site and hauled back in Casey's truck. "We're rock hounds," says Susan, "and we collected a great variety, from sandstone to fieldstone and high-altitude rocks. It's almost like a memory garden. But the farmers usually think you're crazy to want to put in your garden all these rocks they've been trying to get rid of for years."

Placing rocks where they look like they belong is undoubtedly a talent, one Susan finds hard to describe. In her work she's developed a feel for fitting hard objects together, creating pieces from found materials, like the wood-and-springs remnants of an old couch she discovered on the banks of the Athabaska River, and a rusted doll carriage at the side of a highway. "When I work with obscure bits like these I find many of them fit together, even if they come from different places," she says. "This is the way humans fit together in the world. There's a place where everything fits, and there's usually more than one."

With rocks, she says, you get to know them by handling and working with them. "A rock will have a special feature you recognize and want to use," she says. "And when you're working to place two together you'll suddenly know you have a good fit by the sound they make. It will have a nice mellow sound, not just like two rocks hitting each other."

And of course to recreate nature you have to observe it, to really look at it, just as a painter absorbs a scene about to be adapted on canvas. Susan and Casey constantly photograph the things they see on their hikes, from compositions of rocks along a river bed to plants growing together in a community. The vignettes were used as an idea board as their garden was going in.

By the end of the first year the landscape was in place, but the ground was bare. "The neighbors, understandably, were a little concerned because bare ground can attract weed seeds. But that's one reason why I left planting till the

Opposite: The lowered creek bed has rocky banks and a sandy bottom, and it joins a round patio in front of the house. A metal snake mysteriously finds it way from place to place in the bed. Plants are a mixture of native and cultivated species – grasses, creeping thyme (*Thymus praecox*), tall stonecrop (*Sedum spectabile*), pale yellow coreopsis (*Coreopsis verticillata* 'Moonbeam'). Above: Blue Russian sage (*Perovskia atriplicifolia*) and sea holly (*Eryngium*). Below: Dried grasses, stone and driftwood carry the garden through winter.

Above: The pavers of the round patio near the house blend with both the natural rocks and the soft-toned bricks of the house. Blue oat grass (*Helictrotrichon sempervirens*) softens the boundary between a major rock and the pavers. A collection of stones and a pond-in-a-dish sit on a slice of driftwood, joined by a container of plants that includes Million Bells (*Calibrachoa*) a petunia relative.

next year," says Susan. "I wanted to get all the weeds out of the new soil before I started to plant." She put in several varieties of junipers and spruce, a weeping larch, purple-leaf sand cherry, 'Diablo' ninebark, 'Goldmound' spirea and 'Blue Fox' willow, usually in clumps of three or more. Plants include creeping thymes, Russian sage, hostas, daylilies, rudbeckia, purple coneflower and pale lemon coreopsis, arranged in triangles the eye will follow. There are lots of grasses, for winter and summer interest.

The garden was finished in 1999, and except for a couple of new plants that Susan wasn't able to resist, it's stayed essentially the same. She's particularly happy with the way the creek bed works – it actually exists almost as a real creek would in nature, except that it has a limited water source – from spring melt and seasonal rains. "Because we dug right down to the hard clay base under the creek, it retains water," Susan says. "Rains don't drain away as they'd do with a lawn. Then the rest of the garden soaks it up, which means I don't have to water as much as I might have."

Another benefit of her garden: it doesn't make noise. "Often I'm out there just enjoying my garden and the mower across the road starts up, then the one down the street," she says. "We don't stop to think of the noise and air pollution we're causing, or how we're burning all those fossil fuels. If only we would." ■

A "COURTESY WEED NOTICE" slipped through the mail slot by the City of Winnipeg spurred Howard Engel and Esther Juce to finally take out their grass. In the interests of a healthy environment they had refused to use fertilizers, pesticides and herbicides to improve it. The idea for their new garden was the result of a meeting with a grower of prairie plants. A recreated patch of prairie fit their philosophy perfectly because it restored a bit of nature in all its biodiversity; the garden is also drought resistant and requires less maintenance than a lawn or other type of garden, with no need for pesticides.

Howard and Esther took the black plastic route to killing the grass, covering their front yard with 1,000 square feet of it held down with bricks, two-by-fours and rocks. It stayed there for more than a year and wasn't a pretty sight, but no one complained. To minimize puddling on the surface in mosquito-prone Manitoba, holes were poked into the plastic at intervals. When the plastic was removed, the baked grass proved to have become a layer of humus, as promised. Prairie plants were ordered: prairie crocus, cut-leaf anemone, prairie smoke, purple prairie clover, brown-eyed Susans, wild bee balm, New England aster and purple coneflower; plus such grasses as sheep fescue, little bluestem, Indian grass and June grass. Instead of seeding, a slower approach, the couple chose to put in small transplants – more than 1,100 in all.

A landscape architect helped with a planting plan and suggested a few boulders in key places to provide structure and highlight the plants and grasses; she also designed pathways through the plantings for access, even though these elements might not be part of a true prairie landscape. A few existing evergreens such as the 'Hoopsii' blue spruce were left in place as accents.

"After the first winter we had no need to water, and the dead plants return to the soil to feed it," says Howard. "Dragonflies, bees, ladybugs, Monarch butterflies and other good bugs and birds visit us, as well as small animals. Our prairie has taken on a life of its own." ■

The Dandelion Alternative

Winnipeg, Manitoba

The Engel-Juce garden evokes a natural prairie while including practical pathways and a cultivated 'Hoopsii' blue spruce (*Picea pungens* 'Hoopsii'). Rainbow slate quarried in northeastern Manitoba was used because its warm colors reflect the brick and trim of the house, as well as the pavers of the driveway.

Natural Charm

Toronto, Ontario

It isn't necessary to embrace the principles of natural gardening to achieve a warm and welcoming natural look. The owners of the Toronto garden shown here combined a few native plants and grasses with cultivated varieties to achieve an eye-stopping, idiosyncratic style all year round. The grasses swaying gracefully in autumn (middle left and opposite) are left to dry to a golden hue and remain over winter, as seen at bottom left. A couple of deceased annual vines are also seasonal holdovers, kept to provide seeds for winter birds and a lacy look on the porch supports. The firewood on the porch also adds to the natural charm of the downtown garden. In early summer, top left, yellow creeping Jenny (*Lysimachia nummularia* 'Aurea'), sometimes considered an invasive ground cover, combines with a sturdy pink rose, and pink-flowering lamium also hugs the path. ■

Urban and Rural

Natural meadow or prairie gardens naturally fit with homes made of log and stone, such as this Wisconsin house, opposite, where the front yard garden has been planted with nature's own purple coneflowers (*Echinacea purpurea* and *E. pallida*), Culver's root (*Veronicastrum virginicum*), bee balm (*Monarda didyma*) and yellow oxeye sunflower (*Heliopsis helianthoides*). But there's no rule to say that a prairie-style garden won't set off a conventional suburban ranch-style or two-storey home. The rosy beige of the low brick home, above, also in Wisconsin, is complemented by mauve bee balm and pale purple coneflower accented with yellow coreopsis. The Waterloo, Ontario, front garden on the right is made more joyful with an entrance-to-street planting of orange butterfly weed (*Asclepias tuberosa*), mauve bee balm, white Culver's root, yellow cup plant (*Silphium perfoliatum*) and black-eyed Susan (*Rudbeckia hirta*), joined by a white Regale lily and Russian sage (*Perovskia atriplicifolia*), both cultivated species, in the foreground.

Creating the Natural Garden

The kind of natural garden you'll be able to grow depends on the conditions of your site. The essential rule is to observe both nature and your own garden carefully and to choose a natural garden that will work in your space. For example, if you have your heart set on a woodland garden but your treeless yard faces west and has very dry conditions, you're going to have to face facts and start a prairie garden instead.

The next rule is to remember that natural gardening is not an unforgiving religion demanding only the use of native plants, although some might have it so. It's a gardening option, and there's no need to apologize for including hybridized astilbe and hosta with the native bloodroot and ferns in your garden.

Prairies and Meadows

South- or west-facing lots are ideal for sun-loving prairie and meadow plants, and east-facing slopes also work. Leave the northern exposure for ferns and other shade-loving plants. The main requirement is sun, lots of it – an average of five hours a day in summer. Prairie and meadow gardens are drought resistant and adapt to almost any soil – if yours formerly supported turf grasses, prairie and meadow plants will thrive in it.

To decide on what's right for you, find a couple of good native plant catalogs and take the growers' advice. They usually provide growing and design information as well as lists of the plants they sell.

Preparing the Beds

Weed-free soil for planting is crucial, otherwise the existing weeds will compete with prairie seedlings in their quest for nutrients – and probably win.

There are four ways to prepare a weed-free bed:

1. Kill grass with a broad-spectrum, non-persistent glyphosate herbicide. Read the label and follow instructions – it could damage nearby plants you don't want to lose. Apply it three times – in mid-spring, mid-summer and early fall, unless no growth is visible after the second spraying. Then cultivate the bed and wait to see if weeds appear. Remove or use the herbicide again, and sow seeds or put in plants in fall or wait till early spring.

2. Cultivate the plot with a rototiller every two to three weeks over the summer and into the fall, to a depth of four to five inches. Be diligent, or some weeds will recover and begin to grow again. Plant in fall or the next spring.

3. Smother the grass with black plastic or a thick layer of newspaper covered with soil. The vegetation under the blanket will die in a few weeks with either approach, although your neighbors will prefer the newspaper/soil alternative. Then turn over the soil to dig in the dead material, wait for a week or two to make sure no weeds reappear, and plant.

4. The quickest way to get rid of the grass in a small urban garden is simply to remove it. Use a sod cutter or elbow grease to skim it off three inches deep. This usually removes weeds and weed seeds, although the area will be lower than the surrounding planting. But the garden is ready to plant.

Seeds

- Seed may take a year or more to germinate, and up to three years before plants produce bloom. In a small urban garden, it may be better to buy started plants.
- To sow seed, mix it at the rate of one ounce of seed to

three ounces of sand per square foot of garden. Broadcast by hand in a small garden, or use a seed spreader in a large garden.

- Once seed is down, cover it with a dusting of soil to a depth of up to a quarter of an inch. Press seeds down by rolling or stamping the earth or laying boards over it and walking on them.
- Water bed with a fine spray and keep it moist until germination occurs and while seedlings are establishing themselves. Many plants won't germinate for a year or two, so don't be discouraged. You'll continue to be surprised.

Maintenance

- Many growers recommend mowing as a substitute for fires, which have been used to rejuvenate prairie gardens. Mowing in spring removes the previous year's vegetation and cuts back cool-season weeds before they go to seed.
- The first year, set your mower at four to six inches above ground level and mow plants down frequently. This won't hurt the newly emerging prairie plants and will stunt the growth of the undesirables. Remove mowed material so the soil can warm.
- The second spring, mow close to the ground, as close as an inch, and rake off the cuttings. At this point in their growth, prairie plants are still small and won't be damaged by the treatment – in fact, experts in prairie planting say mowing enhances their germination rate.
- If weeds still sprout, mow again in late spring to a height of about a foot. This will set weeds back severely without damaging your emerging prairie plants.
- Don't mow after prairie plants have reached a height of a foot or more.
- Be careful when pulling weeds in the early years of your garden, and avoid it altogether in year one. You could pull up small prairie seedlings along with the weeds. Pulling weeds also dislodges the soil and encourages the germination of new weed seeds.

Prairie or Meadow?

In nature, prairies and meadows are not quite the same, although the French word for meadow is "*prairie*." Both are sunny grasslands containing colorful wildflowers and no shrubs or trees, although trees border most meadows. And therein lies the difference. Meadows exist because of some trauma – a fire or flood, perhaps, even an infestation of pests or disease – that kills part of the surrounding forest, leaving a clearing that becomes the meadow. For this reason a meadow is in transition: within a few years the native tree and shrub species will grow back, filling the area and reverting to forest.

Butterfly weed (*Asclepias tuberosa*) and vervain (*Verbena hastata*) grow on a city boulevard.

Prairies, however, are stable environments – or were, before humans moved in and destroyed most of the tall-grass prairies of the Midwest. They were specific, functional ecosystems that perpetuated themselves through fire and animal grazing.

For the purposes of front yard gardening, the difference is academic and the terms interchangeable.

Planting Tips

- For a good display of wildflowers and to replicate nature, combine them with short clumping grasses like little bluestem, prairie dropseed and side-oats grama.
- Follow the way of nature and plant in sweeps or drifts of one plant. Avoid using only one or two varieties in a garden – you'll end up with a near-monoculture, with the attendant problems of insects and weeds that are attracted to those plants.

Woodland Gardens

A woodland is a subtle expression of nature, a garden of understatement. Look carefully at a natural woodland and you'll see a layered look: a canopy of tall trees shading a lower story of smaller trees and shrubs, which in turn protects a ground cover of low plants. All the layers combine to create a cool, shady retreat that promises peace and solitude.

A woodland garden is the obvious choice for a shady front garden. Plant in masses of one species, such as ferns, trilliums and Virginia bluebells (*Mertensia virginica*).

Woodland gardens have their strongest appeal in spring, when ephemerals (so called because they disappear in summer) such as trout lilies (*Erythronium americanum*), Virginia bluebells (*Mertensia virginica*) and Dutchman's breeches (*Dicentra cucullaria*) bloom madly in tones of white, cream, pink, purple and translucent yellows. Yet somehow there's an implied sense that woodland gardens are second best, not quite as good as a garden basking in full sun that produces an uninterrupted flow of bloom all summer for our satisfaction. But less is more in woodland gardens, where nature provides sheets of a few plants rather than making a big show of many species.

Woodland Garden Guidelines

- Before you plant your woodland garden, visit a woods in your area and photograph plants in their natural setting for inspiration and to get a feeling for their natural placement.
- Woodland gardens in nature prefer friable, humusy soils enriched by the decaying leaves, twigs, bark and nut shells gleaned from the forest around it. Remember this and leave leaves and twigs in place to rot as they will.
- Compost and leaf mulch are good additions to your woodland garden any time. Just spread around plants, no need to dig it in.
- Naturally, woodland gardens prefer shade, although not the deep shade of conifers like pine and spruce. Dappled shade is more to their liking, which may mean limbing up low-branching trees to achieve filtered light.
- Wood-chip or pine-needle paths, ponds and small streams, decaying logs or ancient benches are valuable additions to the design of a woodland garden, as long as they fit the natural look.
- Plant in masses of one species, such as foamflowers or trilliums, and accent them with stands of the more dramatic Jack-in-the-pulpit or lacy maidenhair ferns.
- Small spring bulbs such as glory of the snow (*Chionodoxa*), snowdrops (*Galanthus nivalis*) and checkered fritillaria (*Fritillaria meleagris*) enhance woodland plantings.

Plants

Showy Stuff

black snakeroot (*Cimicifuga racemosa*)
butterfly weed (*Asclepias tuberosa*)
cardinal flower (*Lobelia cardinalis*)
Culver's root (*Veronicastrum virginicum*)
fireweed (*Epilobium angustifolium*)
goldenrod (*Solidago*)
Joe-Pye weed (*Eupatorium maculatum*)
meadow blazing star (*Liatris ligulistylis*)
queen-of-the-prairie (*Filipendula rubra*)
wild ginger (*Asarum canadense*)

Wild ginger

Gorgeous Grasses

big bluestem (*Andropogon gerardii*)
bottlebrush grass (*Hystrix patula*)
little bluestem (*Schizachyrium scoparium*)
prairie dropseed (*Sporobolus heterolepsis*)
sedge (*Carex*)
side-oats grama (*Bouteloua curtipendula*)
sweetgrass (*Hierochloe odorata*)
switch grass (*Panicum virgatum*)

Climbers

American bittersweet (*Celastrus scandens*)
Dutchman's pipe (*Aristolochia durior*)
Virginia creeper (*Parthenocissus quinquefolia*)
virgin's bower (*Clematis virginiana*)
wild grape (*Vitis labrusca, V. rotundifolia*)

Ground Covers

barren strawberry (*Waldsteinia fragarioides*)
bearberry or kinnikinick (*Arctostaphylos uva-ursi*)
creeping phlox (*Phlox stolonifera*)
lily of the valley (*Convallaria majalis*)
pasqueflower (*Pulsatilla*)
prairie smoke (*Geum triflorum*)
spotted geranium (*Geranium maculatum*)
sweet woodruff (*Galium odoratum*)
violets (*Viola*)
wild ginger (*Asarum canadense*)
wintergreen (*Gaultheria procumbens*)

Shrubs

American hazelnut (*Corylus americana*)
meadowsweet (*Filipendula*)
mock orange (*Philadelphus*)
nannyberry (*Viburnum lentago*)
New Jersey tea (*Ceanothus americanus*)
ninebark (*Physocarpus*)
red elderberry (*Sambucus pubens*)
red huckleberry (*Vaccinium parvifolium*)
red osier dogwood (*Cornus sericea*)
serviceberry (*Amelanchier*)
shrub roses
snowberry (*Symphoricarpos albus*)
sumac (*Rhus*)

Purple and yellow coneflowers

summersweet (*Clethra*)
witch hazel (*Hamamelis*)

Good Combinations

butterfly weed (*Asclepias tuberosa*)
pale purple coneflower (*Echinacea pallida*)

creeping blue phlox (*Phlox stolonifera*)
foamflower (*Tiarella cordifolia*)

ferns
trilliums
shooting star (*Dodecatheon meadia*)
mayapple (*Podophyllum peltatum*)

prairie blazing star (*Liatris pycnostachya*)
rattlesnake master (*Eryngium yuccifolium*)

purple coneflowers (*Echinacea purpurea, E. pallida*)
black-eyed Susan (*Rudbeckia hirta*)
yellow coneflower (*Rudbeckia*)
wild bergamot (*Monarda fistulosa*)
Culver's root (*Veronicastrum virginicum*)

wild bergamot (*Monarda fistulosa*)
purple coneflower (*Echinacea purpurea, E. pallida*)
blue vervain (*Verbena hastata*)

Chapter Eleven

Neighborhood Gardens

Gardens of any kind are contagious, but especially front yard gardens. Many neighborhoods are proof of this – for years the fronts of the houses show nothing

more venturesome than velvet lawns and evergreens, then someone widens a foundation planting to fill half the lawn and plants a bed of roses and heathers. The next year, abandoning all inhibitions, the same gardener extends the bed to the street, adding perennials and a pathway, and the next-door neighbor takes the plunge, starting a front yard garden of his or her own. Soon gardens of all kinds are spreading along the street, multiplying like clumps of crocuses, or flinging themselves thither and yon like seeds blown by the wind.

But as with backyard gardens, they're all different, reflecting the personalities and tastes of the owners. The unifying element is their generosity: front yard gardens are shared by everyone who lives in the neighborhood and anyone who passes by. A neighborhood that can boast of a number of them is a lucky neighborhood indeed.

A friendly jumble of bee balm (*Monarda*), rose campion (*Lychnis coronaria*) and lilies, opposite, circle the base of a boulevard tree in front of a Winnipeg, Manitoba, home while rhododendrons and azaleas enliven a narrow boulevard in West Vancouver, British Columbia, above.

TRUE PIONEERS of front yard gardening are rare, and that's one reason why George Tanaka and his next-door neighbor, Rose Haliniak, are so special. George created his garden in 1953, at a time when anything other than perfectly kept grass facing the street was unthinkable. Rose's came a little later, in the early 1960s, and her garden is similar to George's yet different, as we shall see.

George's front garden was unique – a Japanese-style hideaway on a suburban street where gardens front or back with even a hint of an ethnic origin were nearly non-existent. There's another reason why George's garden is unusual: even though he and his wife, Cana, were killed in a car accident in 1982, his garden lives on, close to its original 1950s form, thanks to his brother Kinzie.

"George had a vision," says Kinzie. "He wanted to create a garden that was intimate, with at least one place to meditate, and beautiful from every angle." The fact that it was in the front was secondary, and seemed perfectly natural to George. He'd worked as a gardener in British Columbia before the Canadian government moved his family east during the internment of citizens of Japanese origin in the Second World War. After the family (including Kinzie and his wife, Terry), bought the new ranch-style bungalow in Mississauga in 1952, George was able to take up his avocation again.

"If the neighbors wondered what he was doing out there in the front yard, they didn't ask," says Kinzie. "I guess they were too polite." But a landscape architect who was doing some work in the area stopped by one day and asked George to come to his office for a chat, and the conversation led to a job for George and eventually a degree and a career in landscape architecture.

In the 1950s, when George Tanaka created a Japanese-style hideaway in front of his new bungalow on a suburban street, front gardens were a rarity. The garden is currently maintained by his brother Kinzie, who has divided and replanted many of the original daylilies and ferns.

A Tale of Two Gardens
Mississauga, Ontario

Although George didn't set out to design a Japanese garden, the style naturally evolved, Kinzie says. "He used a lot of gravel, which is synonymous with Japanese gardens, although it wasn't used much in gardens here back then," he says. George also created a typically Japanese raised wood path made of logs planed off on two sides, which were purchased cheaply at that time from lumber yards. These were cut to 16-inch lengths and laid side by side.

"The only trouble with wood is that it eventually rots," says Kinzie, although one path, down the side of the garden, has stood up amazingly well over the intervening decades. The center path didn't survive so well and was regretfully removed by Kinzie a few years ago.

Kinzie admits to a certain amount of angst while deciding how he would replace it, and he eventually chose grass. "There was no grass here at all in the beginning," he says. "Just the wood and gravel pathways, with shrubs and flowers growing right up against them. I didn't want to mess it up." But he's in his late eighties and still does all the garden work himself, and the thought of making a new wood path was daunting. However, now that the grass is in, observes his neighbor Rose, it has to be cared for, mowed weekly in the growing season and clipped at the edge of the flower bed.

Following Japanese design, flowers have a minimal presence in the garden, although Kinzie likes to add annuals he grows from seed for a splash of color. The original

George Tanaka's front garden, created in the early 1950s, was the first in his neighborhood. The garden, peeked into here from the neighbor's driveway, is nearly hidden from the street by a wide band of tall plants including spruce, euonymus and pine.

Behind the dense planting a Japanese-style garden winds its way toward the low ranch-style bungalow, with clumps of daylilies, hostas, ferns and some annuals growing inside raised beds held back with peeled logs.

perennials – daylilies, hostas and ferns – live on, although Kinzie has divided and transplanted them as they matured and the garden's profile changed. The trees (including a cloud-pruned pine in the center of the garden) and shrubs are original, too, diligently cared for by Kinzie to maintain their shape.

The focus of the garden is a nearly invisible pond on the street side of the lot, which is about 65 feet wide including the driveway. To create the intimacy he was looking for, George built a grotto of mounded soil and large rocks topped with evergreens, carefully placed to copy nature. The small pond is hidden on the inner curve, and a viewing bench, a design George created for a park in Stratford, Ontario, was added in the late 1960s. Over the years the

bench, like the plants, has endured, withstanding the elements and growing more beautiful with age.

Rose and Alex Haliniak have been the Tanakas' neighbors since 1952, when they too moved into the new subdivision. But although Rose planted some rhododendrons down the side of the lot and a few birch seedlings across the front, she didn't have time to do much gardening till the early 1960s, after she'd quit work. "I had nothing to do," she says. "And it was a natural thing for me to take up ... I'm from a farming family and gardening is in my blood."

Besides, she says, the grass in the front of the house always looked sparse in summer, and she didn't like the plain exterior of her house. The pear trees on the lot, part of the original orchard the houses were built on, were

One neighborhood garden often begets another, which was the case for Rose Haliniak's garden, shown above. Rose, who lives next to the Tanakas, watched George's Japanese-style garden (opposite) go in during the 1950s, and liked what she saw. In the early 1960s, she had a private courtyard installed with shrubs and small trees to screen it from the street. Her only regret was choosing concrete pavers instead of flagstone for the courtyard floor.

gradually dying. The rhodos had been badly damaged by snow sliding off the roof.

"I'd talked a lot to George about his garden, and watched it go in," Rose says. She liked the privacy and quiet his design provided, but it wasn't quite her style. Then she found a picture in a magazine of exactly the private courtyard she was looking for, with small trees and shrubs planted as a screen near the street, and a flagstone patio near the house. "It was different to George's," she says, "with lots of flowers growing between the stones, very casual."

Even though decades have passed, Rose is still a little disappointed that she allowed the garden center to talk her into concrete pavers instead of the flagstone she really wanted. "I think they made those concrete squares them-selves, or they didn't sell flagstone," she says. "But I'd hired them because they were professionals, and I figured they knew."

Several pavers were left out of the grid pattern to allow Rose to plant annuals in the spaces, some bushy shrubs were added for privacy to the white birch trees she'd planted across the front, and the courtyard was born. "The only criticism we ever had was from a couple of neighbors who thought we were being selfish because we kept our garden hidden from the street," says Rose. "But they weren't really serious."

Every year Rose planted different annuals between the pavers for a change of scene. Then she got smart and put in perennials, which cost less in the long run and required less

Most of the raised wood paths of planed logs laid side by side (above) in George Tanaka's garden lasted for decades, but his brother, Kinzie, needed to replace the center path with grass a few years ago. Rose and Alex Haliniak's garden next door (opposite and below) also evolved, as Rose replaced short-lived annuals with longer-lasting perennials, such as daisies (*Leucanthemum* x *superbum*), coral bells (*Heuchera*) and cranesbill (*Geranium*). Random pavers were also removed to allow for more plants.

work. "For a few years we had a garden full of white daisies, and you should have seen how they glowed at night," she says. "Kinzie would come over and just look at them in awe."

The garden has evolved significantly since it was put in, Rose says. As the years passed she put in more shrubs and took out others. "We never did learn to prune as well as George," she says. "Some of our shrubs just lost their shape." Caring for the flowers became more difficult, so she closed in some of the planting spaces. Plants seeded themselves, even the evergreens and shrubs, and she allowed some to stay, further changing the contours of the garden. "But that's the nice thing about gardening," Rose says. "Plants die out and more spring up. The garden is new every few years. It's up to the gardener to adjust to it." ■

Growing the Gardening Spirit

Winnipeg, Manitoba

ELEANOR THOMPSON'S neighbors paint a humorous picture of her as a sort of gardening angel with a shovel, dropping by after supper with a handful of plants and an offer to help design the new bed they've been struggling with. Kirk Williams jokes that she made suggestions for their front garden before he and his partner, Robert Skene, had even taken possession of their first house on the street (yes, there's a second, but more about that one later).

"That's a big fat lie," says Eleanor with a big laugh, clearly enjoying her reputation. "Kirk and Rob had huge plans for their garden as soon as they bought the house. They'd walk by with their dogs before they moved in and I just asked them exactly what their plans were."

Eleanor is not just curious, she's a driving force behind the gardening spirit in their downtown neighborhood in Winnipeg, Manitoba, says Leslie Sheffield, another recipient of Eleanor's generosity. Eleanor was the first on their street to have a front yard garden, and other streets nearby have since caught the spirit. She organized the weekly walking tours that take place every summer, and she was instrumental in adopting and planting a neighborhood park, using cuttings from residents' gardens and donated plants from local nurseries. "Some people talk about doing things, Eleanor just gets out and does them," says Leslie, who lives across the street.

There was nothing but grass in front of Kirk's and Rob's house when they moved in. "Yes, we did have a plan, done by Rob, who's an architect and knows design," says William. "But we were rookies when it came to plants." Enter Eleanor, soon after they moved in, carrying her

shovel and bags of plants. More neighbors brought tubers and annuals and even a small tree, and a whole army of volunteers had the garden installed in a couple of days, including digging in new topsoil. They also helped put in the new sidewalk and patio of reclaimed brick, and supervised the construction of wood steps and a small front porch, plus an arbor that serves as an entrance to the garden. "The plan changed a bit as the garden went in because there were so many people helping us, " laughs William.

Well, it's that kind of neighborhood. It has a village atmosphere, with people visiting back and forth and sharing barbecue suppers and Sunday morning coffee as well as plant wisdom. Every summer there's a street party, with the road closed for hockey and other games. People garden right down onto the city-owned boulevards, creating beds under the canopy of elm trees that march down the streets. The trees are a Winnipeg landmark, and precious because for years they've been threatened by Dutch elm disease, but they provide more shade than gardeners really like. "We're always having to plant to suit the shade," says Leslie.

But sometimes even the friendliest neighbors like a bit of privacy. In Leslie's front yard garden this is accomplished with a couple of subtle visual messages: a short hedge and a medium-sized conifer placed so that it interrupts the view

For several years, Eleanor Thompson gradually extended the edge of her foundation plantings until – surprise! – she reached the lilacs near the front sidewalk. She did allow a narrow ribbon of grass to remain, mainly in order to tend the tall phlox (*Phlox paniculata*), bee balm (*Monarda*), Oriental lilies (*Lilium*), hostas and impatiens. One of the beds has begun to expand into her neighbor's yard.

from the street of their sitting area. The door-like arbor at Rob's and Kirk's first house, a few doors from a busy thoroughfare that attracts a stream of neighborhood pedestrian traffic, signaled the same message. "Because it was narrow, as opposed to a wide, walk-through pergola, people would pause and ask if they could come in," says Kirk.

What about their second garden? After a couple of years in the first house, the pair decided they needed more space, indoors and out, and found another one seven doors down the street. "We had a garden design down on paper before we moved into this house, too," says Kirk. "But this time we have fewer passersby so we shifted our philosophy – this garden is open and accessible. The paths invite people to walk right in."

The Instant Garden

It took a couple of weekends for Rob Skene, Kirk Williams and their neighbors to put in the garden at their first house. They started with a new pathway of reclaimed brick, the entrance arbor, wide wood steps and a small porch with benches, and the second weekend they converted the plain lawn into a garden oasis. The arbor is a copy of a design by Frank Lloyd Wright that Rob saw in a magazine. The garden plan included a round sitting area near the house, but by the end of the first summer the plants were growing so lushly they spilled over the brick and left little space for chairs. The first year's annuals were eventually replaced with more perennials, plus clusters of potted plants. "Thirty of them," says Kirk. "At first I thought it would be a little over the top, but they looked fine."

The new house, a few doors down the street and bought a couple of years later, has an open yet more "designed" garden (see garden plan, opposite). It's based on two side-by-side circles, one a patio near the house and the other a divided garden near the street, bisected by the street sidewalk. "The design allowed us to expand

Although there was nothing but grass in the front when Kirk Williams and Robert Skene moved into their first home, it didn't take long for the homeowners – with plenty of help from neighbors – to remake the small space. Out went the grass and in went an attractive entrance arbor, designed by Robert, and a path of reclaimed bricks. By the end of the first summer, impatiens, flowering tobacco (*Nicotiana*), petunias and black-eyed Susan (*Rudbeckia hirta*) spilled over onto the walkway.

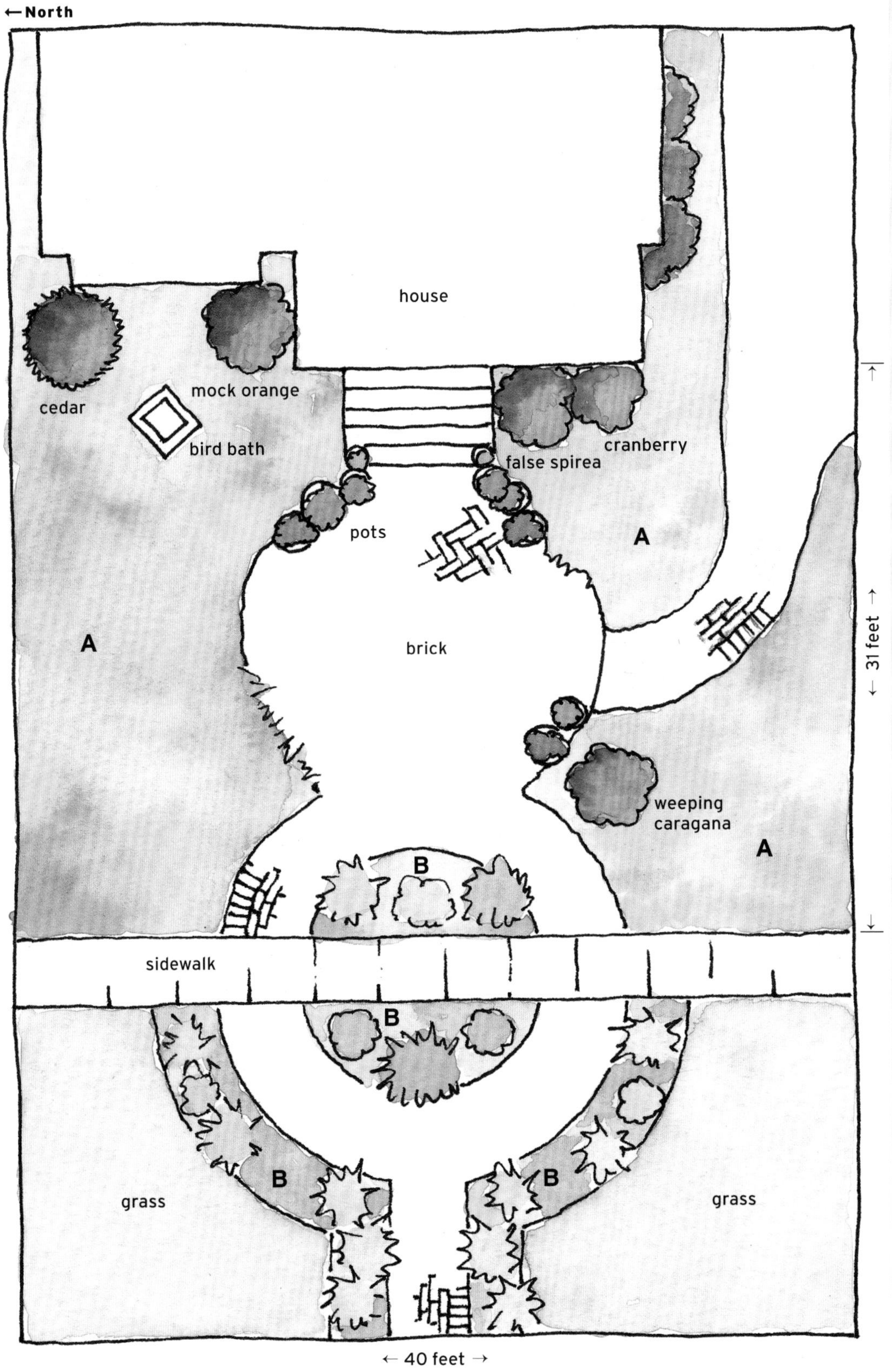

← North

Garden Plan

This is a plan for Rob Skene and Kirk William's second garden; see picture on page 178.

A Mixed plantings of bleeding heart, daylily, Jacob's ladder, phlox, purple coneflower, painted daisy, bergenia, bee balm, Oriental lily, astilbe, peony, plume poppy

B hosta, ligularia, iris, impatiens

house

cedar

mock orange

bird bath

false spirea

cranberry

pots

A

brick

A

weeping caragana

A

B

31 feet →

sidewalk

B

grass

B

B

grass

← 40 feet →

the garden by going down onto the city boulevard, and it's become part of the streetscape," says Kirk. "Kids love that circle – they ride around and around it with their tricycles and wagons, and some of the more unco-ordinated little twerps run right into the plants. But that's okay."

The pathway, planned to resemble open arms that draw you into the garden, was built of reclaimed brick hauled in by the teenage residents of a group home across the street. "We've made friends with them, and they help us with a lot of things," says Kirk. As soon as the path and patio were laid, he and Eleanor jammed the plants in on "one manic afternoon." But he almost had to give up some of his gardening space to Rob's plan. "Originally he had paths on both sides of the patio leading to the backyard – for symmetry, he said – plus paths going into the garden to a bird bath," says Kirk. "We took another look at the plan and I convinced Rob we didn't need two paths going to the back. He knows more about design, and I give in to that, but when it comes to gardening space, that's my territory."

The Little Garden That Grew

Eleanor Thompson loves color and splash, but her new home looked pretty stark when she and her husband and their two-year-old moved in over a decade ago. "The backyard was filled with scrap metal and was just too daunting to tackle, so I decided to start in the front," she says. First she put some shrubs and annuals in to hide the foundation of the house, and began trimming the overgrown lilacs, which are still features of the garden. "I worked hard on them, pruning and shaping to get that look," she says.

"The next year I extended the beds, and every year I'd come out at least another foot. My husband and I have an ongoing joke about how I can never put in an edging because then the garden would have to stop." She'd just take out her shovel and start digging, stopping when the shape looked good.

A couple of years after they finished their first garden, Kirk and Robert moved a few doors away and created a second front garden (opposite; plan on page 177), which also spills on to the boulevard between the street and sidewalk. Their new garden incorporates two side-by-side circles, filled with impatiens, hosta, daylilies and iris, bisected by the city sidewalk. Other gardeners in the same neighborhood create traffic-stopping boulevard plantings (shown above and below) by encircling treasured elms with colorful perennials and annuals.

"The garden really took a jump when I got out to the lilac trees," she says. " I just said to myself, why don't I incorporate them into the bed? So I did, and people going by would say 'Holy Schamoly, what are you doing there Eleanor?' That actually was a turning point on the street, and people started making their beds bigger too."

She did keep a curving grass pathway outside the two large beds flanking the front path, essentially for access to the plants. It sweeps around the front of the lot, inside the cotoneaster hedge and another flower border, and past the wide side bed to the house. The side bed has been extended into the next-door neighbor's yard. "He lets me do what I want because he's not much of a gardener," says Eleanor, happy to get the extra space. Like other gardeners on the street she plants the boulevard too, partly because she can easily see the plants from the house.

Since those first years Eleanor has graduated from annuals to perennials, as many gardeners do, experimenting with varieties that thrive in the shade cast by the street's large elm trees. "Now I'm taking out the ones everybody has and trying more exotic hybrids of things I know grow here, like daylilies and hosta or iris and astilbe."

There is a well-used bench in Eleanor's garden, too. "I'll never be a slave to my garden," she vows. "In spring I do an initial clean-up and some pruning, then I plant the annuals. From then on I just water things, and my neighbor Leslie and I spend a lot of time just sitting and enjoying."

The Sitting Garden

"Our house looked awfully blocky and plain when we moved in, and it had a chain link fence and an 8-foot hedge around the front that my husband just detested," Leslie Sheffield says. "But we had small kids and we didn't do anything about the garden for about six years." That was a decade ago, and then they hired a local nursery to draw up a planting plan, something with curves to soften the lines

When Eleanor Thompson's ever-expanding flower beds (opposite) finally reached her pair of artfully pruned lilacs, it was a turning point for the street. Other people started making their beds bigger, too, she recalls. Above: Neighbors combine efforts to create beautiful borders along property lines, while purple coneflower (*Echinacea purpurea*), double-flowering black-eyed Susan (*Rudbeckia hirta*) and daisies grow at the base of a stately elm, below.

A street-level patio with comfortable seating allows Leslie Sheffield and her husband to visit with passersby and admire their garden. A dwarf blue spruce at a bend in the path creates some privacy; colorful containers line the expansive steps. The contrasting textures of creeping junipers and bergenia in the foreground provide a cool foil for the colorful annuals.

of the house, a patio for sitting. "The elms on the street are so gorgeous, and we like schmoozing with our neighbors, so we wanted to sit out at the front," she says.

At first they considered a porch, but decided they liked the idea of a street level patio because it connected them with the neighborhood. Still, a little privacy was desirable; the designer suggested a dwarf blue spruce in a jog in the pathway leading to the round patio and expansive front steps. It stops the eye just enough to provide a visual barrier. The caragana hedge was like a fortress wall and had to go – at least most of it – but it was not an easy task. "We had to chop the chain link out piece by piece, and then cut the hedge way down," Leslie says. "Now it's just over three feet, just a bit of a screen."

The evergreens are simple but effective because they're planted in masses instead of as single plants, and are combined in different textures and shades of green: creeping juniper, bergenia, and variegated euonymus form the sidewalk bed. Leslie chose classic tall cedars for each side of the large front window because they echo the shutters that were once there. "The clapboard looked so bare when they were gone," she says.

An abundance of potted plants brings big splashes of color in summer. "Eleanor helped me a lot with them," says Leslie. "In the beginning I knew nothing and she was available with advice or cuttings whenever I asked."

The Sheffields' garden is deliberately low maintenance because they have a cottage and are away much of the summer. "But we sit out here every night before supper," Leslie says. "It's such a lovely time of day." ∎

Creating a Neighborly Garden

Just like a smile or a handshake, a front yard garden reveals a lot about its owner in an instant, and it should display perfect manners. That's not to say the garden should be obsessively tidy or overly structured in design, but it should suggest an owner who is considerate of others. Clear access to the house, a generous view of the plantings, attention to weeds and respect of property lines all contribute to a neighborly garden.

Whether yours is the only front yard garden in the neighborhood or one of many, the first thing to consider when planning it are the harder elements visible from the street. The driveway, the path to the door and the front steps are often overlooked, and they send the passerby important subliminal messages.

Paths

The shape of the pathway has meaning. A wide, expansive path that curves gently to the front door says welcome, come on in, and tends to slow foot traffic so visitors can pause and enjoy the surroundings. Straight paths directly to the front door have a more utilitarian or businesslike quality – unless they're softened by exuberant plants spilling out over their edges, as in the lovely sidewalk garden in Cape Cod, right.

The surface materials used on the paths should fit the character of both the house and the garden:

- Brick is a versatile path and patio material: inviting, warm and earthen in color. Laid casually and not too perfectly, it suits a cottage-style house; in a classic herringbone or running bond pattern, rigorously edged, it perfectly fits a grand mansion.
- Flagstone also wears two hats: it's among the most formal of surfaces cut in squares and laid in concrete, but

used as stepping stones in grass or in gravel, it has a natural feeling.

- Commercial concrete pavers masquerade as both brick and stone, and work best with contemporary homes. Most need to age naturally before they adapt to older

This Cape Cod house, with a worn brick path almost hidden by wide, overflowing flower borders, sends a friendly message of welcome to the neighborhood.

Driveway

There's not much you can do about asphalt driveways. They're practical but lack beauty. Gravel looks better, but is too easily tracked into the house. Formal or tumbled pavers could be considered when a change is necessary. In the meantime, allow plants to flow over the edges of the driveway a trifle, arrange a jumble of potted plants near the garage, and even cut out some asphalt so you can insert a few stepping stones where the driveway joins the front walk.

Property Line

A series of gardens in one neighborhood need not be uniform in design. A common thread often develops naturally, especially where gardeners constantly swap plants. But some transition between side-by-side gardens is desirable. One secret of continuity is to use the common areas between gardens.

The neighbors who own the strip of land between their suburban Mississauga driveways in the bottom picture, opposite page, turned it into a traffic-stopper with an expanse of 'Dragon's Blood' sedum that softens the hard look of the asphalt. Even when it's not in bloom, the sedum's texture and flowing growth habit are more attractive than an expanse of flat grass.

Don't ignore the property line. It can be a stark division between your garden and the one next door – especially if it's just a stretch of grass. Here are some ways to deal with it:

- The owners of the tiny strip garden between two modest homes in downtown Toronto in the picture on this page have ignored the property line altogether and bound the two sides together in one garden. It's filled with easy annuals and a few roses, and integrates the homes.
- When a blended garden isn't possible, keep the boundary line soft. If your neighbor isn't a gardener, ask if you can allow your beds to flow over the line in a gentle curve. Most people are happy to comply, as long as you do the work. But if the answer is no, stagger a few loose shrubs on your side of the property line; they'll arch over the boundary gracefully for the right effect.

gardens, although factory-tumbled styles can often pass as reasonable facsimiles of cobblestones.

- Aggregates of small loose stones embedded in concrete look good with starkly modern architecture and simple gardens.
- Pathways of bark mulches, pine needles or even grass suit woodland gardens and simple houses. Raised walks of wood planks or flat logs also lend a woodsy air.

Front Steps

Pay attention to the front steps and entrance pad. Invite people in with wide, shallow steps that encourage a slow ascent, and make sure the stoop is wide enough for at least two people to stand on. Widen it further, and you'll turn it into a small porch suitable for before-dinner drinks.

- Work out a plan to blend your styles. Again, a loose grouping of small shrubs could provide the transition, as could a low clipped hedge, if one of the gardens is formal. A narrow garden-access or postman path could run from one garden into the next, with an arbor tumbling with roses marking the property line.

City Property

Planting the city boulevard, as the owner of the Seattle garden in the picture on the right has done, is one of the nicest ways to welcome passersby and beautify your neighborhood. And contrary to general belief, most municipalities welcome this kind of cosmetic uplift, as long as the garden doesn't impede traffic sight lines.

Just ask – you'll find that the people in charge of boulevards and other public areas, such as highway cloverleafs, traffic calming islands and suburban strip plazas, are only too happy to have volunteers willing to plant otherwise plain grass strips. Sometimes they'll even pay for the plants.

The plantings on these pages demonstrate how gardeners can beautify small areas of shared space that otherwise might be left as expanses of plain green. The gardener at top right shares the boulevard outside his home with the city of Seattle, Washington, and he's planted it bountifully with cannas, red-hot poker and other lush varieties. Right: Mississauga, Ontario, neighbors have planted 'Dragon's Blood' sedum and pink roses to soften the look of their adjoining asphalt driveways. Opposite: Two modest downtown Toronto houses share a simple but exuberant garden of sunflowers, cosmos, alyssum and marigolds, with a red rose thrown in for good measure.

Chapter Twelve

Secret Gardens

Secret gardens were common on the grounds of old European villas and monasteries. Most were walled or hedged formal places with roses and clipped evergreens

arranged around intersecting pathways, where it's easy to imagine the resident countess strolling peacefully, contemplating the afternoon hours away.

It's different in North America. Few of us can boast garden walls, for one thing. But, more important, our garden tradition is not the same. True to our strong work ethic, we too often turn our gardens into places where we labor. If we no longer need to grow vegetables for sustenance we garden to achieve, madly trying to maintain them as perfectly as if we, too, had gardeners to clip the evergreens. Those of us who have learned the lesson of enjoying our Edens tend to tuck a secret space away behind the storage shed or garage in the backyard, where we escape with a book and a blanket (on a chilly day) and are not seen again until dinner is announced at six.

But there's no law that says a secret garden can't be part of the front yard – or even all of it. A small, cozy courtyard can create a warm microclimate for growing exotic species or sitting with morning coffee. A larger one can be a whole experience, with a pond, flower beds and a place for an al fresco supper with friends. Take your inspiration from the gardens and ideas in this chapter: put up a fence, grow a hedge or a wall of shrubs and roses, and create your own secret garden.

Who says a private sanctuary can't be part of the front yard – or all of it? A striking gate, classic floor and the refreshing sound of trickling water contribute to the magic of a secret garden, opposite. The best secret gardens often have a pleasant surprise for visitors – like the jolly Buddha statue beside the dry stream, above. Enclosed courtyards have other benefits, too – they create warmer microclimates, beneficial for more tender plants.

If ALL YOU HAVE is a front yard, you don't have much choice about where the garden goes. But that didn't worry Wayne Renaud when he and Gordon Webber took possession of a rundown coach house in 1986, much against their real estate agent's better judgement.

"It was like a big bowling alley, completely exposed to the street," Wayne says of the lot, which was nothing more than a gravel driveway leading from the street to the coach house, with a mere foot of land behind the house. "But to a designer it was an open palette. I just reversed my thinking and designed a garden for the front."

Rather than trying to divide the long, narrow lot into a garden with a pathway from the street curving around alcoves of planting and areas of use, a common way of dealing with such spaces, he treated it as one big courtyard with a sidewalk straight to the door. House and garden blend so perfectly in every detail that Wayne considers them one big room from the back wall of the house to the garden gate. "In fact, the garden is the heartbeat of the house in every way," says Wayne emphatically.

They were lucky that the entrance to the coach house (which had been occupied as a residence for a number of years, but dated back to 1910 in its original incarnation) was at ground level, with no steps between house and potential garden to separate the areas. The French doors Gordon designed to go across the house did their part to connect the space, too: when they're open on a summer night guests can flow directly from the patio that stretches across the house front into the open-concept living and dining area. The wide second-floor dormer windows also expand

Theme, with Variations
Mississauga, Ontario

real and visual space in the master bedroom, and add style to the exterior of the house.

Because they entertain a lot and operate their business from the house (Gordon designs homes; Wayne is a landscape architect), privacy was as much a priority as was making sure their home was an example of their work, and so walls and fences were in order. "We also wanted a water garden and four-season interest, and we needed a garage," says Wayne. "I think it's worked out perfectly because everyone who comes to the house has to go through the garden. If it was in the back, they might never see it."

The placement of the garage, tucked into the property just off the street, defined the length of the courtyard, 38 feet from the garden gate to the house. (The garage has a charming alcove with a roof overhang and a double-glazed door, and has since become the design studio where the two work; the vehicles are now parked on a paving-stone pad outside the studio.) Wayne designed a gate that has become, in effect, the front door of the house. "It's what we lock when we leave," he says.

The property on which the coach house stands had once been very large, and sections were severed over the years. A house to the south appears to be of 1920s vintage, and the 1940s low-rise apartment buildings behind it have a parking lot that backs onto one side of Wayne and Gordon's garden. On the north side is a large old house of

For Wayne Renaud and Gordon Webber, the front yard is the only garden space they have at their renovated coach house, so they turned the entire area into a courtyard, and designed it as an extension of their living room. Wisteria frames a pair of French doors and the arching branches of a Japanese maple (*Acer palmatum*) anchor one end of the long, formal pond that runs beside the front path to the entrance.

indeterminate age. There were some existing fences, but Wayne had plans for new structures that fit his design.

They approached the neighbor to the north and made a proposal. "But he wanted a pressure-treated fence, so we said we'd build what we wanted on our side and pay for the whole thing," Wayne says. "He wasn't happy and made it very clear – so clear he hasn't let us over on his side to maintain the fence, and it looks like hell now." On that side they erected a 4-foot paneled fence with two-foot pickets above it. On the parking lot side they built a tall stuccoed wall (with the approval of the apartment building's owner), to hide the tenants' cars.

The hexagonal window built into the stucco wall near the house is a good example of Wayne's design philosophy. "I believe in using some kind of rhythm in the landscape," he says. "I like modulating systems that anchor the design." The hexagonal window was rescued from the second floor of the coach house and installed in the wall, where it offers at least the possibility that there's something worth looking at on the other side, even if it's only the branches of a tree. Another original hexagonal window remains in the house, but a new one has been built in the studio wall facing the courtyard to carry out the theme. "I like themes but I like variations, too, because themes strictly adhered to can become boring," Wayne says.

The long, straight sidewalk, itself a style many designers shy away from because it can have an austere effect, was a deliberate design. "The grid of the flagstones was based on the width of the French doors, which happened to be 30 inches, which coincidentally is the size of many precut flagstones. We bordered the flagstones with 6-inch widths of stone, which corresponds with the width between the French doors, and then repeated that in the glass panels down the side of the gate, which total 6 inches with the wood inserts."

The glass panels are turquoise, reflecting the color of the water in the pond, and the pond follows the shape of the sidewalk. But the raised square pond-within-a-pond is skewed to offer a variation on the theme, angled so the

The entrance to Wayne's and Gordon's secret garden is beside the garage (opposite), which defines the length of the courtyard. Every architectural detail was considered, from the color of the bench to the design of the garage trim. Plants were chosen for four-season interest, too, so the view of the garden in winter is as interesting as it is in summer.

Wayne and Gordon chose plants based on their texture and form, as well as color. The feathery plumes of astilbe, above, and the spiky foliage of yellow water iris, below, make a strong statement in their courtyard garden. Opposite is a closer look at the raised square pond-within-a-pond. Water trickles over the edge, pumped from the deeper end near the house, where the koi live.

design doesn't look too uniform as you enter the garden. Cool water trickles over the edge of this pond, pumped from the deeper end near the house, where the koi live. The water in the shallow, gravel-lined end nearest the gate is only inches deep, and Wayne, an aficionado of Japanese design, rearranges the flat stones in it to suit his mood. "Sometimes the stones represent fish swimming in a line upstream, sometimes I cluster them as if they're spawning. It depends," he says.

But he doesn't kid himself that anyone notices the symbolism or the design elements, unless it's the turquoise-gray molding that repeats itself in both design and color throughout garden and house. "Those are subliminal things," he says. "They usually aren't consciously noticed, but they do have an effect on the viewer."

What people do notice is his artful use of plants during all seasons. There's something blooming in the garden in every season except dead winter – when the deep end of the pond remains free of ice, a mysterious pool of dark water – from winter aconite and snowdrops in February to the blue saffron crocus that can appear as late as early December in the protected courtyard. In winter there are berries on the holly and the euonymus, the chocolate vine remains evergreen under the studio roof, the bracts and the bark on the hydrangea look good, and the three varieties of pines at the end of the garden stand out. "They're magical from the upstairs bedroom when it's snowing and you can see the lights of the city reflecting in the sky," Wayne says.

But like all northern gardens, it's wonderful all summer, with wisteria, iris, astilbe, summersweet, ligularia, daylilies and annual salvia and nicotiana providing color and fragrance. At night the fences are lit along their length, casting the plants in silhouette. "People say we've created the perfect landscape," Wayne says, "and I'm inclined to agree." ■

Courtyard, the Movie

Toronto, Ontario

There are times when you hear the story of a garden and it begins to play in your head like a movie, complete with plot twists, characters and drama. So it is with Joe and Paulie Marmina's serene Japanese-style courtyard, a green oasis where stray rays of sun warm strong rocks and the gentle sounds of water disguise the noise of passing cars. Like many good stories, this one delivers a lesson: how change creates opportunity and challenge encourages creative solutions.

The story begins one dark and stormy night nearly a dozen years ago, when lightning hit the family's tree-filled front yard. Joe and Paulie and their four children were devastated to find that one of a group of three gigantic trees had been hit. "It was a huge spruce, and it was down," says Paulie, the storyteller. "It had to come out."

Worse, the downed tree laid bare the sad state of the other trees growing too closely against it, a second spruce and a large maple Joe and Paulie had planted years before when the children were small, so they'd have a place to climb and build a treehouse. They decided to remove both spruces, but although Paulie was heartbroken to see how misshapen and ugly the maple was without its close companions, she wasn't prepared to have it taken down.

"But the day the men came to take out the spruce trees, Joe saw how bad the maple was and told them to cut it down, too," she says. "I came home from work and there was my tree, lying in the middle of the mess. I wept bitterly. The man was all ready to cut it into firewood but I said no, you can't. Just leave it lying there."

After a trip to Japan, Joe and Paulie Marmina decided to turn their front garden into a green, woodsy retreat by adapting some of the elements in the gardens they visited. Rhododendrons, a purple cutleaf Japanese maple (*Acer palmatum*), corkscrew hazel (*Corylus avellana* 'Contorta'), purple-leaved coral bells (*Heuchera*) and a dwarf pine form a serene tableau.

And there the trunk still lies, more than a decade later, beginning to decay but still an integral part of the garden, even its inspiration. For when the trees were gone, Paulie realized they had space for a garden. "We'd been to Japan and liked the quiet and the green of Japanese gardens," she says. "We both like pines and greenery and that loose, woodsy effect, so having a garden like that wasn't hard to agree on. But some other things gave us problems."

The first problem was that they didn't know much about making a Japanese-style garden, so Paulie read up on it. They decided that following the stricter rules of Japanese design wasn't for them, although they would strive for the overall look. To start, Paulie envisioned a narrow sitting deck across the front of the house. "Not one you put chairs on," she says. "But one you put your bottom on and just sit. We'd seen these in Japan and liked them, but I had a little fighting to do because no one else in the family wanted it. But I could see it in my head and I knew it would work."

Once the deck was built, Joe had an idea. "He said we needed something to look at, so we'd better dig a hole and put in a pond," Paulie says. "So it's right outside our door." There was a lesson to be learned from the pond, but it's too late now: it's right under a lovely pine tree. "We didn't plan very well," Paulie rues. "We could spend hours standing out there and catching the needles as they fall into the water. And they make the water really acid." She won't

consider taking the tree down, however – after all, one of the kids brought it home from camp years ago as a seedling.

From the deck and the pond the Marminas – with the help of son Joel, who's been an integral member of their garden team since the beginning – kept moving down the yard with more plans and plantings. "We just winged it," says Paulie. They didn't think much about the plan until they got halfway down the garden and began to notice areas that needed improvement. One was the need for a new path: the existing one was a boring concrete sidewalk that led straight across the front of the house from the garage, and clearly it had to go. To put it discreetly, the plans for a new pathway encouraged some discussion.

"Actually, we had quite a large argument about that," Paulie says. "The Japanese idea is single stepping stones one person can meander along, but my husband said he hated narrow paths and wanted one with big stones two people could walk on together. Joel doesn't like straight lines. Joe likes things neat, and I like plants spilling over the edge of a pathway." So after a few words they got together and made a gracefully curving path that starts at a Japanese-style gate (beautifully made by Joel) halfway down the driveway. The path is made of large, flat flagstones edged with wood chips and controlled planting, and it allowed all three gardeners to have their way.

The fence that encloses the courtyard was another solution to a problem they encountered along the way. A neighbor on one side had an overgrown cedar hedge, and one day Joel suggested they build a fence to hide the dead parts at the bottom. Agreed. "Then another night we were sitting on the deck having wine and looking at the traffic," Paulie says. "Someone commented that when we'd had the big trees we couldn't see or even hear the cars, and why didn't we put the fence across the front, too. The minute it was said we all knew it was exactly the right thing to do."

The fence was built across the lot about two-thirds of the way down from the entrance, creating a cozy enclosure, and a wide planting of evergreens, grasses and ground

After the Marminas built a narrow sitting deck along the front of their house, they realized they needed a focal point, so they added a pond, filled with water lilies, iris and arum. A generous, curving path (below) of large flagstones and pea gravel leads visitors past the pond. Above are the tawny plumes of an ornamental grass.

To reduce traffic noise, the Marminas built a fence across the front (shown opposite), about two-thirds of the way down from the entrance. Sweet woodruff (*Galium odoratum*), hostas and alliums, accented with rocks and stumps, fill the area between the fence and the city sidewalk. Son Joel built the beautiful Japanese-style gate, above. Below is a glimpse of the old, dead maple trunk – the impetus for the garden – surrounded by ornamental grasses, including Japanese blood grass (*Imperata cylindrica* 'Red Baron').

covers, accented with rocks and wood stumps, was installed inside the fence. It fills the garden on one side of the new pathway and rhododendrons, azaleas, evergreens, a weeping mulberry and a Japanese maple grow on the house side. And this is where the old maple trunk came into its own. "I suddenly saw a dry stream bed running from the path to the side fence," Paulie says, "with the log, left where it was, making it look like the stream was coming from under the path and flowing under the log to the fence." The log became a focal point as well as a keepsake.

A few years after the courtyard was completed (it took a couple of summers), the Marminas decided to create a garden outside the fence for the benefit of passersby. It features an extension of the stream bed, with river stones and boulders that appear from under the fence, fooling the eye into thinking it originates with a stream bed inside. "But it doesn't really connect with the stream bed inside," confesses Paulie. "That one goes in the direction of the driveway, but this one picks up at the fence and goes toward the street." Well, okay – a bit of artistic license has been taken with the setting, just like in the movies.

Even the three huge limestone rocks that dominate the street bed are a dynamic part of the story. Joe, Paulie and Joel agreed they wanted two perfect specimens as show-pieces to set off the outer stream bed, and Joe and Joel drove to northern Ontario on a hunt. They found what they wanted, one in the shape of a whale. The truck arrived, and as the crane was putting the whale into place, it fell and broke in two. "Joe was really mad," Paulie says. "He demanded a refund. But it's a funny thing – it turned out that three stones looked better than two ever would have."

Stanley Kubrick couldn't have scripted it better. ■

Simple and Sophisticated

A tranquil Toronto courtyard, walled in for almost complete privacy, is a frequent gathering place before dinner parties in the rear garden, which overlooks a ravine, as well as a quiet spot for the owners' morning coffee. The extended stones in the limestone walls mimic a style frequently used by architect Frank Lloyd Wright in the 1930s, while also reflecting the cantilevered structure of the modern house. The teak insets in the wall allow breezes to find their way in to the sunny courtyard, which has a small pond and rock fountain almost hidden in one corner to help disguise noise from the street. The clematis and Australian fan flower used as a bedding plant guide the way from the driveway into the courtyard, where border beds spill over with a blue, pink and white color scheme of more fan flower, white tuberous begonias and pink impatiens. Plantings are kept to the sides of the terrace to allow space for visitors, and lushly planted earthenware pots add more color to the plan.

The Cottage Gate

The low lattice gate above, in West Vancouver, has a simple presence that adds a geometric touch to the informality of the garden tumbling over and around it. Essentially it's more cottagey in mood than the gate below, but the straight lines and subdued design, combined with the classic doorway revealed beyond the gate, result in a restrained effect.

The Dramatic Gate

A handsome gate can make a statement about any garden, even if it isn't hiding a secret space. It implies there's something wonderfully mysterious and inviting on the other side – especially if the door is ajar, as it is in the garden on the left, also in West Vancouver. Gate and fence have an unusual color scheme and an uncommon combination of materials that work perfectly to underline the character of both house and garden: the delicate ironwork of the gate reflects the green of the plants tumbling over the fence, and the gray-blue painted wood matches the shingles of the house and echoes the stone embedded in the risers of the concrete steps. The roof over the gate also suggests the owners care about the comfort – and dryness – of their visitors.

Creating a Secret Garden

Although the enclosed gardens profiled in this chapter are relatively spacious, allowing room for a stroll or a dinner party, secret gardens are often small. Many people like the idea of a small entrance courtyard: it's like an antechamber to the front door, a spillover place where you can say good-night to guests or have your morning coffee in privacy.

Depending on where they're sited, small courtyards can create microclimates warmer than the rest of the garden, allowing the gardener to grow plants that would normally survive only in a zone or two higher, or to protect plants from a particularly windy situation.

Small gardens are also fun to design (see Chapter Six for more ideas). Larger enclosed gardens should be designed like any other front garden, but remember to take advantage of the backdrop provided by the wall, hedge or fence, especially when considering the view from the house. Bigger courtyard gardens can also offer warmer, more protected microclimates just inside the wall or fence.

Floor

Small courtyards don't lend themselves well to grass because they're difficult to cut. You could use a whipper snipper, of course, but why waste such a potentially charming space on grass? Try a low ground cover you can step on instead, such as thyme or vinca. More practical are hard surfaces like flagstone, brick, gravel or even wood planking.

Walls

Without something to enclose it, a garden wouldn't be secret. The garden wall isn't common in North America, but if your neighbors agree and your municipality allows, one could certainly be built. Hedges are soft and organic, but good ones take ages to grow. Fences are the quickest – just be sure they aren't forbidding. Check the height regulations in your district.

- Lovely walls can be made with concrete blocks covered with stucco. A narrow box made of plywood can also

Concrete blocks covered with stucco make an elegant wall. Check municipal bylaws for height restrictions and provide a strong foundation to prevent damage from frost. Finishing details, such as peek-a-boo windows and attractive coping, add polish.

serve as the base for a stucco finish, like the one in Wayne Renaud's garden in this chapter. Be sure to set walls in strong concrete foundations below the frost line, and top with flashing or a cap to keep out moisture.

- Use the wall of an extended garage – the kind often seen attached to large suburban houses on small lots – as one side of an entrance courtyard.

- Plain wooden fences can be given personality with trellis work painted a contrasting color and hung on hooks an inch or so away from the fence to create shadows or hold vines.

- *Trompe-l'oeil* trellis patterns are also effective, and don't let the French intimidate you. It simply means an optical illusion, in this case slats set at an angle, in a receding perspective, making it look like an arbor or alcove set in the fence. You could also paint a landscape or set a mirror into the center to suggest there's more there than a fence.

- Store-bought lattice panels make good fences and allow the breezes through. For variety, combine diagonal and square lattice, open and privacy weaves, or panels of lattice and solid wood. Soften the look further with a rampant growth of vines.

- With any wall or fence, heed the details: battens covering solid boards add a finishing touch, as do decorative moldings and bracing pieces placed by design rather than by chance.

- Grow a nearly instant hedge on industrial wire mesh, using the quickest-growing evergreen vine hardy in your area. If you have a modern house, the mesh will look perfectly appropriate even while the vine matures.

- Hedges can look good as they grow. Start with plants as big as you can afford, plant them well in deep trenches and good soil, and keep them clipped so they're always well shaped and have a finished look. They'll gradually evolve from low, decorative walls to tall ones offering complete privacy.

Water

- There's nothing more soothing outside your door than the sound of water softly falling from a tap or other decorative source on the wall into a basin below. A still pond is easier, though without the sound effects: fill a handsome big pot with water and float a fragrant hardy water lily (*Nymphaea odorata*) in it.

- Place a bird bath in the courtyard, or attract butterflies with a low dish filled with sand soggy with water and topped with a flat stone. In the garden, don't forget a few plants the butterflies love.

Focal Points

- A small window cut into the fence or hedge enclosing a large garden can offer a glimpse of a borrowed view and a sense of mystery.

- Keep a small courtyard simple and concentrate on one desirable focal point – the water feature, a good piece of sculpture or urn overflowing with plants, a bench or a chair and side table.

Euonymus and clematis soften the wall behind a pond while koi dart under the leaves of water lilies, adding to a contemplative mood.

Plants

Fragrant Plants

Plants with scent are a priority in a secret garden. Here are some suggestions. Check with your local nursery for those hardy to your area.

Michigan lily

Annuals

flowering tobacco (*Nicotiana alata*)

heliotrope (*Heliotropium arborescens*)

mignonette (*Reseda odorata*)

moonflower vine (*Ipomoea alba*)

night-scented stock (*Matthiola longipetala* subsp. *bicornis*)

sweet alyssum (*Lobularia maritima*)

sweet William (*Dianthus barbatus*)

Perennials

Chinese wisteria (*Wisteria sinensis*)

daffodils (*Narcissus*)

dame's rocket (*Hesperis matronalis*)

freesia (*Freesia*)

hyacinth (*Hyacinthus*)

Japanese wisteria (*Wisteria floribunda*)

lemon daylilies (*Hemerocallis lilioasphodelus*)

lily of the valley (*Convallaria majalis*)

Michigan lily (*Lilium michiganense*)

sweet violet (*Viola odorata*)

tuberose (*Polianthes tuberosa*)

Shrubs and Trees

brugmansia (*Brugmansia*)

daphne (*Daphne*)

gardenia (*Gardenia augusta*, G. *thunbergia*)

honeysuckle (*Lonicera*)

jasmine (*Jasminum*)

lilac (*Syringa*)

linden (*Tilia*)

mock orange (*Philadelphus*)

Russian olive (*Elaeagnus angustifolia*)

summersweet (*Clethra alnifolia*)

viburnum (*Viburnum*)

Lemon daylilies, and pansies

Overcoming Obstacles

The people on the following pages may not live for a challenge, but they know how to rise to one, even in the garden. Deep slopes, up or down (shallow ones can

actually be a nice change of scene); cars, ever-present in our lives today; fire hydrants demanding center stage on tiny lots; telephone poles where you don't want them; yellow painted curbs that say don't-park-here-but-please-look-at-me – all these are rife in front yards. And they need to be addressed, not ignored, for a successful front yard garden.

For example, the owner of the small house on this page loves her garden but has to deal with the overpowering presence of a car, as many small-lot suburban and city dwellers do. The only space for it was in the front, and she decided that since she couldn't disguise a parking pad, she would integrate it with the house. Thus, it has a surface of crushed red stone that matches the house but blends with the garden, which – small as it is – surrounds the parking space and takes over the view.

The gardener managed to work with the problem of a small lot and a front yard parking spot to create a harmonious garden. This chapter provides other examples of people who have used their ingenuity and creativity to overcome obstacles in their front yard gardens.

Opposite: Stone steps and terraced beds with spirea, ivy, yellow tulips, variegated red-twig dogwood (*Cornus alba* 'Elegantissima') and birch accent a steeply sloped yard. Above: A gardener with a small house and big driveway lessened the driveway's impact by using crushed red stone that blends with the garden.

STEEP SLOPES may be great in a vineyard, but they're a challenge for a gardener, says Josie Szczasiuk. "Actually, my garden is very Canadian," she says. "Extremely hot in summer and freezing in winter." The south-facing slope captures heat and also makes spring come early and fall stay late, which can be a welcome bonus. Sometimes the soil has thawed so completely in February that Josie can dig and plant. "But when winter comes, plants used to such warm conditions often aren't ready for it. I've had a hard time finding things that can survive such extremes of temperature and don't qualify as weeds."

The garden, which at the front door is about 18 feet higher than the street, 40 feet away, presents a couple of further challenges: it has sandy soil that drains off rainwater almost the instant it lands, sometimes resulting in near-drought conditions. There's also an evergreen hedge on the street boundary that traps the cold air and frost that roll down the slope, creating a frigid microclimate when the rest of the garden may be reasonably temperate. But Josie chooses not to consider these as problems. "They're challenges," she says. "If you look at the conditions in your garden as problems, you're going to be an unhappy gardener."

She's also learned to view her garden as a collection of microclimates, and to deal with it in sections, rather than treating it as one entity with hot, dry summers and cold winters. "Tree roots and shade, for example, can affect a particular area's conditions," she says. "I think too many people, especially new gardeners, try to go at the whole garden at once, as one piece. Then they get very stressed if things don't work and they drop out."

The south-facing, sloping garden captures heat and extends the seasons at both ends. Neatly clipped cones of yew frame the pretty teal door, while tall iris, sea kale (*Crambe cordifolia*), variegated euonymus and pinks (*Dianthus*) soften the edges of broad steps. The shallow steps and generous landings make the steep ascent a pleasant experience.

High and Dry

Toronto, Ontario

When Josie and her husband, Mark Abbott, moved into their west-end Toronto home about fifteen years ago, the front yard was mainly lawn. Josie would have been happy to leave it that way and garden in the back, but an attack of white grubs changed her plans. "The grubs made me do it," she says with a laugh. "We kept replacing patches of dead grass with sod, but we were just providing a kinder, gentler environment for the grubs, so we moved on to something else."

Since the steps leading up through the front yard provide the only access to the front door, extending and reinforcing them was a priority. A former owner had installed nine steps up from the street, leveled the land slightly to make a gradual slope for the lawn, and then continued the rise to the house with a rock garden and a few stepping stones. It had to be made safer, says Josie.

"Scattered flagstones are a devil of a thing to shovel in winter, and we didn't want to send our newspaper guy flying. So we augmented the stones with wider and deeper ones and cemented them in place." They also added an iron railing at street level, and lighting to make for safer evening access. Originally Josie also put in an access path of stepping stones to reach the plants she was putting in, but they've disappeared in the subsequent growth.

So has the original rock garden. "The only reason I can guess it's there is that I see the stones embedded in the soil, but the yews have taken over," Josie says. This was fine with her – the yews and some other evergreens and the hedges were all part of the original garden and they give the garden some "bones" and the house some privacy. Besides, Josie was busy trying out plants that would do more than merely survive in her garden, but at the same time wouldn't require coddling. "My original plan was to have an alpine tapestry. Extreme conditions, on a slope – it sounded like just what you'd need for alpines. Well, yeah…. That didn't work."

Neither did the thymes many people recommended. "I've never been able to establish a full square yard of thyme here," she says. "Thymes grow in mounds and hillocks. Even the miniature varieties won't mat out for me. And they suffer lots of winter dieback."

Josie believes in having fragrance and color by the front door, where there's a small terrace for sitting, so there she's planted daphne, witch hazel, fragrant spring bulbs, Japanese maple and dogwood, which fill the bill nearly all year round. In the rest of the garden she's tried to keep plants low, but if something tall does well, it's welcome to stay, such as the pretty purple and white bearded iris or airy *Crambe cordifolia* (which is very like baby's breath). It may seem obvious to long-time gardeners, says Josie, but gardening is a learning experience, and many people expect too much too soon. "You have to develop an attitude of trial and error, and if something doesn't work you check it off your list and go on to the next thing." ∎

Plants: Josie's Choice

Here are some tried and true dependable plants that survive beautifully in Josie Szczasiuk's garden of extremes, yet require little care.

Trees
'Cherokee Chief' flowering dogwood (*Cornus florida* 'Cherokee Chief')
cornelian cherry (*Cornus mas*)
crab apple (*Malus*)

Evergreens
compact fragrant viburnum (*Viburnum farreri* 'Nanum')
compact mugo pine (*Pinus mugo* var. *pumili*)
cotoneaster (*Cotoneaster apiculatus*)
creeping juniper (*Juniperus horizontalis* 'Wiltonii')
euonymus (*Euonymus fortunei* 'Emerald Gaiety', *E. fortunei* 'Kewensis', *E. fortunei* 'Emerald 'n' Gold', *E. fortunei* 'Sarcoxie', *E. alatus* 'Compactus')

false cypress (*Chamaecyparis obtusa* 'Nana Lutea')
Scotch pine (*Pinus sylvestris*)
'Sunkist' cedar (*Thuja occidentalis* 'Sunkist')
yew (*Taxus*)

Shrubs
'Arnold Promise' witch hazel (*Hamamelis intermedia* 'Arnold Promise')
Burkwood daphne (*Daphne x burkwoodii* 'Astrid')
February daphne (*Daphne mezereum*)

Perennials
'Autumn Joy' sedum (*Sedum* 'Autumn Joy')
border phlox (*Phlox paniculata*)
bugleweed (*Ajuga reptans*)
columbine (*Aquilegia*)
common Solomon's seal (*Polygonatum x hybridum*)
cranesbill (*Geranium*)

iris, mixed bearded varieties (*Iris germanica*)
pinks (*Dianthus*)
rock rose (*Helianthemum*)
rugose roses (*Rosa rugosa*)
sea kale (*Crambe cordifolia*)
woolly speedwell (*Veronica spicata* subsp. *incana*)

Bulbs
crocus (*Crocus*)
drumstick allium (*Allium sphaerocephalon*)
'Lutea Maxima' fritillaria (*Fritillaria imperialis* 'Lutea Maxima')
tulips (*Tulipa*)

Lavender and purple-edged white iris and magenta cranesbill (*Geranium*) contrast beautifully with the backdrop of formal, dark green evergreens.

MOST GARDENS adjoining houses that undergo major renovations require some kind of repair or redesign, but Michael and Michelle Binkley's presented more than your average challenge. For one thing, their lot sloped steeply down from the street at the front to Burrard Inlet at the back, with the house roughly in the middle of its 200 foot depth and vulnerable to drainage problems. There were two sets of existing stairs: one straight down the middle with a landing of asphalt paving to allow you to catch your breath on the way up, and a second set down one side. "Carrying stuff out was brutal, but even taking in groceries was awful," says Michelle.

Michelle and Michael are both artists who work at home, and solving the drainage and stairs challenges were not their only priorities. Michael, a stone sculptor, needed a large, flat area where he could display some of his outdoor works at the popular twice-a-year shows the couple hold at their home studio. Michelle, a flower designer who specializes in romantic bouquets, arbors and church decorations for weddings, wanted a place where she could satisfy her need to grow beautiful flowers and demonstrate her own artistry. She also wanted to grow textured foliage to use in her arrangements.

The couple planned well for the challenges of their garden. In 1997 and 1998, as their modest house was converted into a handsome studio gallery, they worked out a plan to deal with drainage and display. An arc-shaped plateau would be created at the top of the 50-foot-wide lot, forming two grassy arms that would become the display

The Artists' Garden

Vancouver, British Columbia

area. This grassy arc would be retained on each inner side with dry-laid stone walls inspired by the freestanding stone walls on sheep farms in Ireland. Two paths, one to accommodate stone stairs and the other a gentle slope of flat stones to allow wheelbarrow and wheelchair access (for visitors to the gallery), would curve down on each side of the excavated area and meet at an enclosed courtyard near the front door, then veer off to each side of the house, diverting water away from the house and into side beds.

Grading the earth to create The Promontory (the name they gave to the main display area) was part of the agreement with the contractor. But as soon as the earthmover left, another problem raised its challenging little head. "Like complete idiots, we hadn't put any money aside for hard landscaping," says Michelle. "After the contractor left us with the excavation, we were on our own. We had to beg, borrow and steal to get all those rocks for the terracing."

Worse, they had to do most of the work themselves, except for a couple of family weekends when guests were invited to help dry-lay some of the stone. "It took us nearly two years and about sixty trips in our pickup truck to bring back some free hunks of basalt, which we found along a highway to Whistler." They also fell heir to a couple of pieces of curved granite from a broken bridge, which have become part of the retaining wall around the stepped portion of the entranceway.

Michelle and Michael Binkley's steeply sloping lot in North Vancouver presented serious drainage problems. They also needed a large, flat area where Michael could display the stone sculptures he makes. Their solution: a plateau at the top of the narrow lot and two paths – one with steps, the other sloping to accommodate a wheelbarrow – curving down to the house. Dry-laid stone walls retain the inner sides of the two paths and provide a warm microclimate for plants.

After the excavation, Michelle and Michael were left with the job of terracing the paths and laying the retaining walls. "It took us nearly two years and about sixty trips in our pickup truck," Michelle says. Above: Iris, yellow fumitory (*Corydalis lutea*), chives and foxgloves spill over the rocks. Below: Michelle designed the swirling pattern for the courtyard's floor, while Michael created the rectangular fountain. Water trickles through the gray-blue pebbles laid on the granite top, which is set on a basalt base. Opposite: The garden is the perfect setting for Michael's stone sculptures.

The concept of a dry-laid retaining wall sounds simple enough: choose rough-edged rocks rather than smooth, round ones, lay them on top of each other tightly, finding ones that fit together well, and as you work lean the wall backward, into the earth. Farmers have been making similar walls or fences for centuries. "But it's harder than it looks," says Michelle. "You really have to make sure the rocks are secure, and you have to maintain the integrity of the slope. It was harder for us because we got the stones for free and beggars can't be choosers. We worked with what we had and didn't need to cut any of them – although who would have been better to do that than a stone carver with a diamond saw? But I would never recommend uneven stones like these ones. They should be more uniform and flat."

The wall has stood the test of nearly five years without a serious flaw. "Although it's settled in a few places and we've had to dab in concrete here and there near the top, if only because we open the gallery a few times a year and it has to be safe at all times," Michelle says. Drainage hasn't been a problem, either – as planned, water from the upper level gently finds its way down the two stone paths and falls away to each side of the house, except for one little area where it sometimes collects. "But by the time we discovered the problem it was going to take a big outlay of money to fix it, and it's really not too bad," Michelle says. "The water drains away completely in six or seven hours, and according to the research we've done it would be a serious problem only if it stayed for twenty-four."

In the beginning, Michael and Michelle considered putting in an underground watering system, but they got an estimate and realized they just couldn't afford it. So they wound black drip hoses through the beds and connect them to the main line when the garden needs water. The curving rock walls automatically provided both shady north-facing spots (where Michelle grows her beloved hostas) and hot southern exposures. She has great success with rosemary, which can be temperamental about staying alive all winter even in Vancouver's usually balmy climate, and lavender, which wantonly spills out of the walls' crevices. "I also have

yellow winter jasmine, which grows like crazy out of the wall. I'm always trimming it back," Michelle says.

Planting pockets in the wall hold poppies and saxifrage near the base, blue lithodora and violas farther up, and corydalis and aubrieta near the top, where plants tend to dry out because water drains away from these areas first and they generally receive the most sun. Michelle says she learns more every season about what grows successfully and what doesn't do well in rock walls.

The garden's design is essentially Michelle's, including the lovely swirling pattern in the floor of the square courtyard. "The pattern doesn't mean a thing, I just liked it," she says. The big pieces are slabs of granite, and the 3- to 5-inch rectangular ones are sandstone trimmed to fit, all sunk into gravel. The modernistic rectangular courtyard fountain was one of Michael's creations, made of two pieces of basalt fitted together for the base, with a slab of granite laid horizontally for the top. Water is pumped up through the basalt base to the midpoint of the granite behind the gray-blue pebbles, where it slowly emits. Michael carved the granite so a barely perceptible flow of water oozes over its surface and over the edge, then down the basalt base, offering a gentle dripping sound.

Visitors who come to see Michael's work love Michelle's garden and its cheerful, free-form plantings of cottage-style flowers, which also change as the years pass and the plants overgrow their designated spots. "My problem is that I plant things really close together because I don't like to see the soil," she laughs. "The pressure comes later, when you have to move them to a new spot." ■

The courtyard leading to Michelle and Michael's front door is square, and the lovely stone wall was erected by the builder as part of the contract. Once it was up and the grading of the lot was finished, the couple were on their own to complete the rest of the garden. "Woman Eating Grapes," seen in part at left, is one of Michael's sculptures.

Plants for Rock Walls

Plants like succulents love the heat and arid conditions of a rock wall, with their tops in the sun and their roots next to cool stones. If there is shade, ferns and hostas will be happy at the base, where moisture might collect. Small vining plants are appropriate for the center or top, where they can tumble down the warm stone. But be sure you don't plant an invasive or large vine, such as Virginia creeper or silver-lace vine: it could take over and be difficult to pull out. The dry areas at the top of the wall are suitable for Mediterranean plants and herbs such as sage, lavender, hyssop, rosemary and chives. Watch for wilting during dry periods, and water your wall generously from above.

Plants for sunny, dry walls
basket-of-gold (*Aurinia saxatilis*)
big root cranesbill (*Geranium macrorrhizum*)
creeping Jenny (*Lysimachia nummularia* and *L. nummularia* "Aurea', which has chartreuse leaves)
creeping mazus (*Mazus reptans*)
creeping speedwell (*Veronica repens* and *V. pectinata*)
donkey tail spurge (*Euphorbia myrsinites*)
dwarf lady's mantle (*Alchemilla erythropoda*)
maiden pinks (*Dianthus deltoides*)
rock cress (*Aubrieta*)
stonecrops (*Sedum acre, S. spathulifolium, S. oreganum*)
succulents, for example: hens and chicks (*Sempervivum*)
thymes, especially low-growing varieties (*Thymus praecox* 'Pseudolanuginosus', *T. serpyllum, T. praecox* 'Coccineus' and 'Purple Carpet')
violas (*Viola*)
wall cress (*Arabis*)

The Sore Thumb Syndrome

A bright fire hydrant is never going to fade into the landscape, so you might as well incorporate it into the design. The owner of the tiny Toronto garden above has played up its presence by following through on its bright yellow color with a row of marigolds. The balance of the plantings (roses, blue lobelia and sweet alyssum) are muted pastels, leaving the yellow to dominate.

The owner of the slightly larger space above uses the live-and-let-live philosophy, treating the hydrant as a necessary presence if not quite a piece of sculpture. The graceful, carefully pruned pine tree, limbed up to allow light into the garden below, is the garden's focal point, but the hydrant contributes its own personality to the scene. The garden is planted with ferns, fibrous begonias, impatiens, sedum and golden creeping Jenny (*Lysimachia nummularia* 'Aurea').

You can also capitalize on ugly bits like telephone poles and yellow curbs, often a blight in suburb developments. Do as the Wisconsin gardener in the photo above did when dealing with the don't-park-here-please or this-is-a-dangerous-curve yellow line: plant a predominantly yellow garden to match the yellow paint: daylilies, black-eyed Susan (*Rudbeckia hirta*) and golden marguerite (*Anthemis* x *hybrida*).

The photo above shows how a gardener in Unionville, Ontario, disguised a weathered telephone pole with a garden of its own: a large bed of shrubs and tall plants with an arbor and a bird house. The pole hasn't disappeared, but it's the garden that catches your eye as you drive down the street. The plants around the pole are tall orange daylilies, Shasta daisies, delphinium, roses and ferns.

The Circular Drive

It can be a practical solution to lots of visitors arriving en masse in lots of cars, or it might reveal a yearning for the days when big money meant a big driveway right to the portico over the front entrance. Nevertheless, a circular drive will dominate the space unless it's handled with finesse. Here are three attractive solutions.

Left: Huge new modern residences can seem intimidatingly nouveau riche, but here's one with a feeling that somebody who likes plants and people lives inside. The garden has a distinctly formal style, as befits the style of the house, but because it fills the island in front of the house it pulls the eye away from the starkness of the asphalt driveway. Nothing but grass in this area would be less than welcoming. The garden is a European-style formal balance of upright conifers, hostas, a trimmed boxwood hedge and variegated euonymus. The greenery is centered by an urn planted with licorice plant (*Helichrysum petiolare*) and petunias, which are echoed in the urns to each side of the front door. Hydrangea standards grow on each side of the garden's central urn.

Opposite, top: This contemporary, sophisticated approach doesn't deny the need for vehicular access to within a few feet of the door, but acknowledges that an entrance should reflect some character and sense of pleasure. This is difficult to bring off, but it's been done with a few plants and lots of style in this garden with a soft gravel driveway, a fence with an open, welcoming arm (painted to match the gravel and the paneling on the house) and a cheery planting of white Shasta daisies (*Leucanthemum* x *superbum*) and pink geraniums.

Opposite, bottom: The large, casual Ottawa garden here disguises the driveway beautifully — so well that it disappears from view at the street, as it does in this picture. Glorious foxtail lilies (*Eremurus*), lady's mantle (*Alchemilla mollis*), roses, sundrops (*Oenothera fructicosa*) and shrubs fall all over each other to welcome visitors, and reflect the owner's warm personality.

Yes, We Have a Car or Two

On a big lot one can house a few cars and a big garden as well. The Winnipeg garden here is a good example: it boasts an island bed to the side of an unabashed driveway. The garden is filled with wild plants: bee balm (*Monarda*), purple coneflower (*Echinacea purpurea*), black-eyed Susan (*Rudbeckia*) and goldenrod (*Solidago*).

A wonderful bird bath sits on top of an old stump. The cars, however many there are, can boldly occupy the driveway and parking area without distracting from anyone's appreciation of the garden. The secret in a space as large as this is to be bold with the garden, and hang the cars.

Picture Credits

All photos are by Andrew Leyerle unless otherwised noted below.

Karen Bussolini: 112, 114, 115, 123, 128, 130, 132, 183
Corbis: 11, 20
Janet Davis: 25
Christopher Dew: 191, 192 top, 193, 203, 204
Elliot Erwin, Magnum Photos: 16
Bert Klassen: 187, 196, 197 bottom, back cover author photo

Manulife Financial: 27
Marilynn McAra: 47, 111, 116, 119, 124, 133, 152, 154, 155, 156
National Trust Photographic Library, Rupert Truman: 8
Richard Palanuk: 166, 179, 181
Jerry Pavia: 110, 120, 121
Jane Braddock Peticolas, Courtesy of the Thomas Jefferson Foundation Inc.: 13
Liz Primeau: 29, 30, 32, 33, 34
Suzanne Scott: 42, 52 top
Rose Stepanko: 127, 134, 136

Bonnie Summerfeldt: 39, 99, 135, 177
Kirk Williams and Robert Skene: 176
Paddy Wales: 93, 104, 167, 202, 212, 214, 215, 216, cover bottom right
Warshaw Collection of Business Americana, Archives Center, National Museum of American History, Smithsonian Institution: 13

Gardeners

The gardeners were generous with their stories and their pictures; however, some preferred to remain anonymous. A big thank-you to all the gardeners for their hard work and the creativity that made this book possible.

Gardeners are listed in order of their first appearance.

Liz Primeau: cover top left, 29–40
Suzanne and Michael Scott: 42, 43, 50–54
Judith and Peter Adam: 46, 79, 80
Tammy Sage: 49, 74, 81
Ferne Taylor: 56, 62–65
Liza Drozdov: 57–61
Anne Kotyk: 66, 67
Brenda Simmons and Peter Chisholm: 68
Claudia Matesa: 69 top
Betsy Miller: 69 bottom
Patrick and Patti Hurley: 71
David Lee and Peggy Karfilis: 72 bottom, 158, 159
Susan Lewthwaite: 73 top, 184
Theresa Weindl: 82, 83
Dennis Reid: 84 left, 205 bottom
Lorraine Johnson and Andrew Leyerle: 85

Robert H. Desmarteau: 86 top left
Carol Bujeau: 86 top right
William Boyle and David Montgomery: 89
Kathy Farrell in consultation with Be-Leaf: 91
Dorothy and Julio Durdos: 72 middle, 92, 100–103
Hazel and Gerry Van Slyke: cover bottom right, 93, 104
Dianne Dietrich: 94, 96–98
Barbara Mitchell Pollock: 105
Lee and Ross Jamieson: 111, 116–119
Gordon White: 112–115, 123
Malle and Peter Nagy: 126, 138, 139
Rose Stepanko and Barry Lastiwka: 127, 133–137
Jan and John Trimble: 128–132
Peter Fowler: 141
Howard R. Engel and Esther G. Juce: 144, 151
Norma Lounsbury: 145
Helen McKean: 146–50
Susan and Casey Como: 152–156
Ron and Kathy Jaworski: 161 top
Anne and Allan Morgan: 161 bottom
Wilinksi: 160
Douglas Counter: 163

Bill Walter: 167
Kinzie and Terry Tanaka: 168, 170, 172 top
Rose Haliniak: 171, 172 bottom, 173
Eleanor Thompson and Barry Miguez: 174, 180
Kirk Williams and Robert Skene: 176, 178
Leslie Sheffield: 182
Clayton Antieu: 185 top
Mary Fitzgerald: 185 bottom
Wayne Renaud and Gordon Webber: 186, 188–93, 203, 204
Paulie and Joseph Marmina: 187, 194–199
Elaine Carrey: 200
Clare Philips: 202 top
Val Marshall: 202 bottom
Susan Summerville: cover top right, 206
Susan Mills: 207
Josie Szczasiuk and The Growth Group: 208, 211
Michael and Michelle Binkley: 212–16
Cally Bowen: 218 left
Mei Yung Fong: 218 right
Dale and Jeanette Winkler: 219 left
Allison Scott: 221 top
Rebecca Baker: 221 bottom
Robert and Judy Stewart: 222, 223

Sources and Recommended Reading

SOURCES

I used many sources for the information in this book, particularly for Chapters One and Two, and only the major ones are listed below. I'm dazzled by the number of web sites available offering information about the safety and hazards of pesticides; however, the subject is so complex that even a thorough surfing of the net won't provide a definitive answer to a concerned gardener.

Some of the design advice I offer was gleaned through my own years of gardening, and much of what's in my head was picked up through reading magazines and books, watching television gardening shows and listening to the advice of other gardeners. I wish every source could be credited.

p. 14: Quote from Frank J. Scott, *The Art of Beautifying Suburban Home Grounds*, 1870.

p. 14: Quote from Frederick Law Olmsted from *Second Nature: A Gardener's Education* by Michael Pollan, Atlantic Monthly Press, 1991.

p. 15: Quote from Robert Fulford, "The Lawn: North America's Magnificent Obsession," in *Azure* magazine, July/August, 1998.

p. 22: Description of nylon weed-trimmer: *Changing Times*, March: 1980.

p. 22: Thatch-o-matic advertisement from *Horticulture* magazine, September 1976: 51.

WEB SITES

http://www.hc-sc.gc.ca/pmra-arla/english/pubs/rev-e.html

http://www.kanataenvironmentalnetwork-com/facts.html

http://www.turva.me.tut.fi/iloagri/pest1/pest2.htm

http://www.24d.org

REFERENCE BOOKS

Arthurs, Penny. *Small-Space Gardens.* Madison Press. Toronto: 1997.

Billington, Jill. *Really Small Gardens.* Quadrille Publishing Limited. London: 1999.

Bormann, F. Herbert, Diana Balmori and Gordon T. Geballe. *Redesigning the American Lawn: A Search for Environmental Harmony.* Second edition. Yale University Press. New Haven: 2001.

Hayward, Gordon. *Garden Paths.* Camden House Publishing. Charlotte, Vermont: 1993.

Jenkins, Virginia Scott. *The Lawn: A History of an American Obsession.* Smithsonian Institution Press. Washington: 1994.

Keen, Mary. *Gardening with Color.* Octopus Publishing Group. Markham, Ontario: 1991.

Stein, Sara B. *Noah's Garden: Restoring the Ecology of Our Own Backyards.* Houghton Mifflin Company. New York: 1993.

Teyssot, George, Editor. *The American Lawn.* Princeton Architectural Press, with the Canadian Centre for Architecture, Montreal. New York: 1999.

Really Small Gardens. Jill Billington. Quadrille Publishing Limited. London, England. 1999.

RECOMMENDED READING

I have three shelves of gardening books, and all of them have value. But some I refer to again and again – for a good read or for advice. These are my favorites.

Arthurs, Penny, Brenda and Trevor Cole. *Creating a Garden.* Madison Press. Toronto: 1996.

Brookes, John. *John Brookes' Garden Design Book.* Dorling Kindersley. London: 1993.

Clausen, Ruth Rogers and Nicolas H. Ekstrom. *Perennials for American Gardens.* Random House. New York: 1989.

Hogue, Marjorie Mason. *Amazing Annuals.* Firefly Books, Toronto: 1999.

Johnson, Lorraine. *100 Easy-To-Grow Native Plants.* Random House of Canada. Toronto: 1999.

Keeble, Midge Ellis. *Tottering in My Garden: A Gardener's Memoir.* Camden House. Toronto: 1989.

Keen, Mary. *Decorate Your Garden.* Conran Octopus. London: 1993.

Kennedy, Des. *Crazy About Gardening: Reflections on the Sweet Seductions of a Garden.* Whitecap Books: Vancouver: 1994.

Lima, Patrick. *The Harrowsmith Perennial Garden.* Camden House Publishing. Toronto: 1989.

Mitchell, Henry. *One Man's Garden.* Houghton Mifflin. New York: 2003.

Index

Erysimum cheiri (wallflower), **63**
Erythronium (trout lily), 108, 164
Eschscholzia californica (California poppy), 38, **41, 72,** 73, 91
Euonymus, 37, 125, **170,** 192
  E. alatus (burning bush), 41, 66
  E. a. 'Compactus,' 41, 66
  E. fortunei (variegated euonymus), 182, **208,** 210, **220**
  E. f. 'Emerald Gaiety,' 78
Eupatorium maculatum (Joe-Pye weed), 38, **146,** 147, 165
Euphorbia (spurge)
  E. myrsinites (donkey tail spurge), 217
  E. polychroma (cushion spurge), 33, **37, 40,** 41, 109
evergreens, 89, 108, 125, 182, 198, 209–10, 220. *See also individual species*

fairy moss (*Azolla*), **97**
Falk, John, 10
false cypress (*Chamaecyparis*), 210
false indigo, 148
false strawberry (*Duchesnea indica*), 143
feather grass (*Stipa tenuissima*), **130**
fences
  in cottage gardens, 70
  for courtyard gardens, 191, 197, 203, 204
  in opulent gardens, 95, 106
  in prairie gardens, 147
  in small city gardens, 86, 89
fennel (*Foeniculum vulgare*), 73
ferns, 82, 118, 169–70, 217, **218, 219**
  in cottage gardens, **63, 64,** 70
  holly, 114
  Japanese painted (*Athyrium niponicum* 'Pictum'), 125
  maidenhair (*Adiantum pedatum*), **123,** 125, 164
  in natural gardens, **145, 164,** 165
  sword (*Polystichum*), 55
  tree (*Cyathea arborea*), **82**
  wood (*Dryopteris*), 55
fertilizer, 24, 26, 63
Festuca (fescue grass)
  F. glauca (blue fescue), 41, 88, 125
  sheep fescue, 157
Filipendula (meadowsweet), 165
fireweed (*Epilobium angustifolium*), 165
flagstones, 47, 183
flowering almond (*Prunus triloba*), 55
foamflower (*Tiarella cordifolia*), 66, 109, **125**
  in natural gardens, **145, 164,** 165
focal points, 89–90, 91, 106, 204

Foeniculum vulgare
  'Atropurpureum' (bronze fennel), 73
forget-me-not (*Myosotis*), 67, 72, **75,** 138
fountain grass (*Pennisetum setaceum*), 109, 129–30
fountains, 67, 90, 217
Fouquiera spendens (thorny ocotillo), **110**
four o'clock (*Mirabilis jalapa*), 73
foxglove (*Digitalis*), **72,** 86, **214**
Freesia, 205
Fritillaria, 164, 210
fumitory, yellow (*Corydalis lutea*), **214,** 217
fungicides, 102. *See also* pesticides

Gaillardia (blanket flower), 109
Galanthus nivalis (snowdrop), 72, 108, 164, 192
Galium odoratum (sweet woodruff), **126, 138,** 143, 165, **199**
garden furniture, 70
Gardenia, 205
Gardening Success with Difficult Soils (Ogden), 129
garden plans, 39, 99, 135, 177
gardens. *See also specific geographic locations; color schemes; container gardening; dry stream beds; planning*
  accessories in, 70, 82–83, 90, 124
  bog, 99
  boulevard, 176–79, 185
  costs of, 52–55
  for dry conditions, 111, 129–31, 157
  English-style, 101–5, 129–31
  for extreme conditions, 209–10
  eyesores in, 218–19
  focal points for, 89–90, 91, 106, 204
  hard elements of, 45–47, 111, 153–54, 203–4
  history of, 111
  Japanese-style, 88, 111, 123, 169, 195–98
  lighting for, 45, 55, 102, 192, 209
  maintaining, 163
  northern, 99, 117–19, 133–37
  organic, 24
  planting, 37, 150, 155–57
  prairie, 88, 144, 147–51, 157, 161–64
  preparing beds for, 155–57, 162
  professional help for, 44, 51–52
  rock, 51–52
  seeding, 162–63
  shade in, 64, 115, 164, 217
  statuary for, 70, 106, 215, 217
  styles of, 88, 89
  in winter, 155

woodland, 164, 184
garlic (*Allium sativum*), 73, 88
gates, 197, 202
Gaultheria procumbens (wintergreen), 108, 165
Gaura lindheimeri, 41, 72
gayfeather. *See Liatris*
Geranium (cranesbill), **46,** 80, **138, 172, 210, 221**
  G. cinereum 'Ballerina' (dwarf magenta geranium), **98**
  G. macrorrhizum (big root cranesbill), 217
  G. maculatum (spotted geranium), 165
  G. sanguineum (bloody cranesbill), 72
Geum triflorum (prairie smoke), **37,** 41, 88, 157, 165
gillyflower. *See Matthiola*
ginger, wild (*Asarum canadense*), 165
gladiolus, 82
glory of the snow (*Chionodoxa*), 108, 164
glyphosphate herbicide, 150, 162
goatsbeard (*Aruncus*), 55, 72
godetia. *See Clarkia*
golden chain tree. *See Laburnum anagyroides*
goldenrod (*Solidago*), 109, 147, 150, 165, **222–23**
golf courses, 14–15, 20
goutweed (*Aegopodium*), 86
grape hyacinth (*Muscari*), 33, **37, 66,** 134
grape (*Vitis*), 165
grass, 88, 129–30, 155, 157, 158, 164. *See also* lawns; *individual species*
  Bermuda, 13
  big bluestem (*Andropogon gerardii*), 165
  blue fescue (*Festuca glauca*), 41, 88, 125
  blue oat (*Helictrotrichon sempervirens*), **156**
  bottlebrush (*Hystrix patula*), 84, 165
  buffalo (*Buchloe dactyloides*), 20, **128,** 129–30
  creeping bent, 26
  dormancy of, 20–21
  feather (*Stipa tenuissima*), **130**
  fountain (*Pennisetum setaceum*), 109, 129–30
  hakonechloa, 125
  Indian, 129, 157
  Japanese blood (*Imperata cylindrica* 'Red Baron'), 125, **198**
  June, 157

Kentucky blue, 13
  little bluestem (*Schizachyrium scoparium*), 20, 125, 157, 164, 165
  muhly (*Muhlenbergia*), **128,** 129, **130**
  native, 13–14, 20
  ornamental, 41, **47,** 125, 165
  prairie dropseed (*Sporobolus heterolepsis*), 88, 148, 164, 165
  reed (*Calamagrostis*), 98
  ribbon, 118
  St. Augustine, 130
  sheep fescue, 157
  sweet (*Hierochloe odorata*), 165
  types of, 13–14, 15
  zebra (*Miscanthus sinensis* 'Zebrinus'), 96
gravel, 123, 169
  in driveways, 184
  for dry stream beds, 118
  as mulch, 90, 111, 115, 121
  in paths, 47, 84
ground covers, 55, 86, 87, 122, 142–43, 165
Gypsophila (baby's breath)
  G. paniculata, 72, 137
  G. repens (creeping baby's breath), 33, 41, **71,** 134

Hakonechloa macra 'Aureola' (golden variegated hakonechloa grass), 125
Haliniak, Rose and Alex, 169, 170–72
Hamamelis (witch hazel), 96, 165, 210
Hamilton, Ontario, 82–83
hazel. *See Corylus*
health hazards, 21, 22–23
Hedera (ivy), 70, 122, **206**
  H. helix (English ivy), **52**
  H. h. 'Baltica' (Baltic ivy), 55, **142**
hedges
  in courtyard gardens, 203, 204
  in formal gardens, 89
  in neighborhood gardens, 175–76, 181–82
  in opulent gardens, 106
Helianthemum (rock rose), 33, 41, 125, 210
Helianthus annuus (sunflower), 73
Helichrysum petiolare (licorice plant), **220**
Helictrotrichon sempervirens (blue oat grass), **156**
Heliopsis helianthoides (oxeye sunflower; false sunflower), 107, **160**
Heliotropium arborescens (heliotrope), 73, 108, 205
Helleborus orientalis (lenten rose), 109

stock (*Matthiola*), 73, 108, 205
Stokesia laevis (Stokes' aster), 109
stonecrop. *See Sedum*
stones
  as accents, 129, 131, 155, 157, 198
  for driveways, 113–15
  in minimalist gardens, 123–24
  for paths, 45–46, 47, 78, 129, 183, 209
  for retaining walls, 78, 81, 213–17
  in rock gardens, 52
succulents, 217
sumac (*Rhus*), 148, 165
summersweet (*Clethra alnifolia*), 67, 165, 192, 205
sundrop (*Oenothera fructicosa*), **221**
sunflower, **184**
  false (*see* sunflower, oxeye)
  Helianthus annuus, 73
  Mexican (*Tithonia rotundifolia*), 73
  oxeye (*Heliopsis helianthoides*), **107**, 160
Sutera cordata (bacopa), **86, 89**
sweetgrass (*Hierochloe odorata*), 165
sweet pea (*Lathyrus odoratus*), 73
sweet potato vine (*Ipomoea batatus*), **86**
sweet rocket (*Hesperis matronalis*), 72, 205
sweet woodruff (*Galium odoratum*), **126**, **138**, 143, 165, **199**
Swiss chard (*Beta vulgaris*), 88
switch grass (*Panicum virgatum*), 165
sword fern (*Polystichum*), 55
Symphoricarpos albus (snowberry), 165
Syringa (lilac), **56, 64, 65**, 179–81, 205
  S. meyeri 'Palibin' (dwarf Korean lilac), **127**, 133–34, **134**
Szczasiuk, Josie, 209–10
Tanaka, George and Cana, 169–72
Tanaka, Kinzie and Terry, 169–72
Taxus (yew), **208**, 210
Taylor, E.P., 17

Taylor, Ferne, 63–64
Thalictrum (meadow rue), **58**, 125
thatch, 22, 26
Thompson, Eleanor, 175, 179–81
Thuja (cedar), **71**, 118, 210
Thunder Bay, Ontario, 105, 140
Thymus (thyme), 41, 108, 118, 122, 143, 210
  T. x citriodorus (lemon thyme), 143
  T. x c. 'Silver Queen' (silver thyme), **115**
  T. praecox (creeping thyme), 33, 90, **154**, 156
  T. p. x 'Coccineus,' **141**, 143, 217
  T. p. 'Pseudolanuginosus' (woolly thyme), 137, **141**, 143, 217
  T. p. 'Purple Carpet,' 217
  T. serpyllum, **141**, 217
Tiarella cordifolia (foamflower), 66, 109, **125**
  in natural gardens, **145**, 164, 165
Tilia (linden), 205
Tithonia rotundifolia (Mexican sunflower), 73
tobacco, flowering. *See Nicotiana*
tomato, **73**
Toronto, Ontario, 66–68, 95–99, 138–39, 158–59, 184, 195, 218
  small city gardens in, 77–81, 84, 89, 91
Trachelospermum asiaticum (Asian jasmine), 129, 131
trees, 122, 125, 205, 210
Trifolium repens (white clover), 143
Trillium grandiflorum (trillium), **75**, **145**, 164, 165
Trimble, Jan and John, 129–31
trout lily (*Erythronium*), 108, 164
tuberose (*Polianthes tuberosa*), 205
Tulipa (tulip), 41, 55, **75**, 108, 210
  in fusion gardens, **126**, 133–34, **138**
  species, 72
  T. 'Arctic Flame,' **40**
  T. bakeri 'Lilac Wonder,' **38**
2,4-D, 19, 23
Unionville, Ontario, 219

Vaccinium parvifolium (red huckleberry), 165
valerian (*Centranthus ruber*), 73
Valerianella locusta (lamb's lettuce), 73
Vancouver, British Columbia, 105, 167, 202, 213–17
Vandermeer, Asbjorg, 117–18
vegetables, 73, 82, 88, 105
Verbena
  V. bonariensis, 91, **104**, **110**, **120**
  V. hastata (blue vervain), **163**, 165
Vernonia (purple ironweed), **146**, 147
Veronica (speedwell), 134
  creeping, 217
  V. spicata (spike speedwell), 109
  V. s. subsp. *incana* (woolly speedwell), 210
Veronicastrum virginicum (Culver's root), 147–48, 150, **151**, **160**, **161**, 165
Versailles, France, 10
vervain. *See Verbena*
Viburnum, 205
  V. farreri 'Nanum' (compact fragrant viburnum), 67, 210
  V. lentago (nannyberry), 165
Vinca minor (periwinkle), **46**, 108, 122, **143**
vines, 131, 217
  in natural gardens, 158, 165
  in small city gardens, 82, 90
Viola odorata (sweet violet), 205
Viola (pansy), 98, **107**, 217
  V. x wittrockiana (icicle pansy), 72, **87**, 91
Virginia bluebell (*Mertensia virginica*), **126**, **138**, 164
Virginia creeper (*Parthenocissus quinquefolia*), **140**, 165, 217
virgin's bower (*Clematis virginiana*), 165
Vitis (wild grape), 165

Waldsteinia fragaroides (barren strawberry), 165

wall cress (*Arabis*), 217
wallflower (*Erysimum cheiri*), **63**
walls
  courtyard, 191, 203–4
  retaining, 78, 213–17
Wasowski, Sally and Andy, 129
water features, 90, 204. *See also* fountains; ponds
water lily (*Nymphaea odorata*), **196**, 204
Waterloo, Ontario, 161
Webber, Gordon, 189–92
weeds, 22, 25
Weindl, Teresa, 82–83
White, Gordon, 113–15
wild ginger (*Asarum canadense*), 165
wild grape (*Vitis*), 165
Williams, Kirk, 175–79
willow, 80, 156
Winnipeg, Manitoba, 157, 167, 175–82, 222–23
winter aconite (*Eranthis hyemalis*), 96–98, 108, 192
wintergreen (*Gaultheria procumbens*), 108, 165
wiring, 45, 55
Wisconsin, 147–50, 160–61
Wisteria, 90, **188**, 192
  W. floribunda (Japanese), **34**, 58, **84**, 205
witch hazel (*Hamamelis*), 96, 165, 210
wooden paths, 47, 169, 184
wormwood. *See Artemisia*
Wright, Frank Lloyd, 176, 201

xeriscaping, 110–11, 121
yarrow. *See Achillea*
yew (*Taxus*), **208**, 210
Yucca, 88, 125

Zea mays (corn plant), 82
zebra grass (*Miscanthus sinensis* 'Zebrinus'), 96
Zephyranthes (rain lily), 115
Zinnia, 73, **128**, **131**